Vermin:
A Traveler's Bestiary

Marilyn Stablein

Spuyten Duyvil
New York City

ISBN 978-1-947980-67-9

Library of Congress Cataloging-in-Publication Data

Names: Stablein, Marilyn, author.
Title: Vermin : a traveler's bestiary / Marilyn Stablein.
Description: New York City : Spuyten Duyvil, [2018]
Identifiers: LCCN 2018031033 | ISBN 9781947980679
Classification: LCC PS3569.T127 A6 2018 | DDC 813/.54--dc23
LC record available at https://lccn.loc.gov/2018031033

CONTENTS

Six: Winners & Losers

One
Street Show

MIGUEL

The city of Pelangro is the second largest in the province. Every winter, a week before Independence Day, a circus comes to the central plaza. In two days a tent is erected, all the caged, trained animals unloaded, and the enormous rope nets and high-wire swings are set up. On the third day the show opens.

I want to join one of the circus acts, but the manager Miguel told me to come back when I'm thirteen. Sometimes I go to school, but mostly I work for Miguel who says what I do for him is good training for the circus. We started begging together in the streets, downtown, as the evening crowds filed out of the office buildings.

It's easy to pity a man without legs, a rubber bathmat tied under his torso and a girl in rags. We always chose a deserted place, so Miguel would not get trampled; he figured that people needed to see him from fifteen feet away so they would have time to consider his plight before they passed.

Eventually Miguel outgrew pity. He manages a traveling street show now. I'm in one of the acts. We move around the outskirts of Pelangro every three weeks in four large pushcarts, unpack our sandwich boards in another vacant lot, and begin again. I'm glad we don't travel to other cities; I can still go to school if there is one nearby. Sometimes I stay with an aunt but I usually stay with Miguel in his cart.

We can't compete with the real circus—no sense trying. Miguel says that people are tired of the same old acts: bearded ladies, snake charmers, and sword-swallowers. I think he's right.

"Awe or horror," Miguel says, "that's what people will pay for. That's what brings them back. Our show has to be good. By good I mean grotesque."

Rat Circus

Jose owns the rat circus. He used to be in business for himself but he joined Miguel's sideshow about three months ago. He simply pushed his cart next to the others and added his name to the painted signs.

One side of his cart is glass so the audience can see the elaborate tunnel network, the merry-go-rounds, Ferris wheels, and treadmill that trigger a chute that drops corn kernels one by one over the rats' heads—that's how they eat.

On the three wooden sides of the cart Jose painted pictures of the Rat God copied from his village temple up north. At one time rats were worshipped for their cunning and fertility before the famine and before the plague and before the missionaries taught that the rat was an instrument of the devil. Many people still believe in the Rat God, a rotund deity decked out in jewels.

Jose's prized attraction is Raheno, a caged albino rat that many believe is related to the Rat God himself. Peasants will pay the entrance fee to our show just to bring tasty morsels to feed the albino rat.

His glassed-in area is barely large enough for him to turn around in. His sole activities are eating and sleeping. As a consequence he's grown enormously fat.

Every so often Raheno goes into a spin, circling and circling the cage that is only a few inches larger than his bloated body. The glass gets steamy with his panting. He spins and spins until he collapses on his side, swollen rib cage heaving, his disfigured head dizzy and limp. Villagers, thinking Raheno's spin is an auspicious divine omen, place bets on the frequency and duration of his frequent spells. One urchin boy gets a few coins when he alerts others about Raheno. As soon as he sees the rotund albino rat circling his cramped cage trying to bite his own tale, he'll run through the village streets shouting:"Raheno is spinning! Raheno is spinning!"

Villagers are quick to pick up on the news. Soon from one shack to the next the cry goes out: "Raheno is spinning! Raheno is spinning."

THE BOTTLED WOMAN

Miguel gets credit for designing this act. He purchased a giant, long-necked bottle from a soft drink company that was switching from bottles to cans. The bottle is eight feet tall and once stood atop the soft drink factory. The opening is just wide enough for a thin, naked girl to squeeze through.

I am the thin, naked girl. Inside I can barely stand up. I prefer to sit cross-legged even if my knees are scrunched against the sides of the bottle. The thick glass magnifies my body, like an optical illusion, making me look like a woman except for the breasts.

After I squeeze in, the top is sealed with a giant cork. I breathe the air that is trapped inside and can stay corked up for an hour at most.

At first I just sat in the bottle. Then Miguel filled the bottle three-quarters full with water so I had to tread water to breathe. Now he changes the act every week.

One week Miguel puts in two snakes. They're harmless but I hate the way they slither beneath me looking for a dark nesting place. Another week Miguel will drop in cockroaches. He pays some street urchins *cinco centavos* for a dozen. They bring him shoeboxes full of tree roaches, the large variety.

When I'm cooped up with the roaches I keep my eyes shut and pretend they're something else: leaves, butterflies, ladybugs. Miguel gives me a swig of whiskey before I squeeze in.

Once he tried ants. He poured a sugary solution over

my skin to attract them then dropped in a bucketful of ants. They were the country variety, very small, very quick. It took them half an hour to crawl over my body. They swarmed over every inch. I had to suck in air between my teeth so I wouldn't get a mouthful. Ants crawled in my ears, up my nostrils making me sneeze. They sucked on the moisture in my eyes and elsewhere. Fortunately the crowds didn't go for it. They had trouble seeing the ants through the thick glass. No one believed there were ants covering my body.

"She has dark skin," a man shouted. "You can't fool me!"

"Those are ants, you fool!" Miguel countered."Look closer. You're blind."

After that Miguel ditched the ants. He kept the act popular by alternating the snakes with the roaches.

The Shit Swallower

"Throats and cunts." Miguel said. "Think of the horrible things you could cram down or force up those slimy crevices."

It was a Saturday night and we were sitting around overturned apple crates. The men were playing cards, smoking cigarettes.

"And I don't mean swords or fire or spikes or diseased pricks," he continued. "Think of something dreadful...a violation of some sort..."

He was trying to elicit ideas since we needed new acts. I don't remember who first suggested shit or if it was even suggested in a serious way.

"That's perfect," Miguel said. "Shit. Why not? It's repulsive. It's disgusting. It's perfect. I know people will pay."

The men drew straws to see who would not have to swallow shit and Carlos lost. At first they thought they could fake the shit. But they discovered very quickly what they already knew: shit is unique. No matter how hard you tried to duplicate it, you couldn't. You could borrow the smell, but the consistency, the color, and the texture was impossible to reproduce. So Miguel needed to use the real thing.

Carlos tried to back out. But after Miguel got out his whip Carlos relented and agreed to try it, especially if he could count on a reasonable percentage of the take.

Next they had to decide what shit Carlos would eat: cow shit, dog shit, squirrel shit—God, there was a lot of shit to choose from. They argued and argued until finally Carlos stood his ground.

"If I'm going to eat shit," he proclaimed, "it'll have to be good shit, high-class, that is. Absolutely no exceptions."

"What in the hell is high-class shit?" Miguel asked.

We all knew what low-class shit was like. Carlos was silent for a moment.

"Baby shit," he replied. "From a baby not yet weaned from the mother's breast. That would be high-class." I admired his vision.

Word went out that Miguel, manager of the Street Show, would pay for good-quality baby shit. At first the mothers laughed so hard tears came to their eyes. But when they realized they could actually get cash for their babies' shit, you should have heard the bickering.

"Healthy shit," one claimed, "has the consistency of pudding."

"No it doesn't," another argued. "It should be pasty, like my baby's. Not liquidy." Still another mother claimed that firm round pellets were perfect for eating.

One said that her vegetarian diet produced the sweetest milk and, in turn, the sweetest shit. Scrunching up our noses, we each looked closely at the samples. Finally Miguel chose the vegetarian and sent the others away.

Next Carlos had to practice eating. At first he had to put salsa over the stuff to try and disguise the taste but he soon got used to nibbling it raw. He stopped gagging and his eyes stopped weeping.

For his act Carlos sat at a table covered with a white cloth. He wore a white cotton shirt with a tie, and used a large white napkin and a silver spoon. I played a toy drum, beginning with a soft rumbling and building to a tumultuous crescendo.

Miguel wooed the crowds: "Ladies and gentlemen," he began. "You are about to see the world-famous star, the modern sensation, the undisputed one and only, irreproachable human SHIT SWALLOWER !!!"

Miguel belted out his spiel from a newly designed pedestal that raised his torso up so people thought he had legs like everyone else. To attract people and convince them this was a real act we placed a particularly smelly pile of shit underneath the platform between the wheels.

Then I rattled on the drum to get attention. Next I ducked behind Carlos and swept a large palm leaf fan back and forth, ostensibly to keep the flies away but really to circulate the stench. The pile had to be changed daily because of the maggots; we took turns providing a refill.

People paid twenty centavos to see the show. Soon the Shit Swallower act was wildly popular. We had to set up benches of flat boards balanced on empty crates in front of Carlos' table. Crowds lined up for a chance to sit in the front row.

Poor women brought their nursing babies. "Don't you ever grow up to be a Shit Swallower," a mother warned her baby.

Rich people came by on their way to the temple. If anyone stayed for two acts I turned the drum upside down and walked through the rows passing the drum like a church collection plate to get more money.

The take was good for two months but then slacked off.

"What's wrong?" Miguel demanded of Carlos. "You're losing your touch."

Maria reported that two competitors had appeared in

town and that one even sold dried specimens, church-approved, of a priest's shit. It was said to be a cure-all.

Carlos beefed up his act. He began to prepare the shit in different ways: he sliced shit patties; he gargled some with water; he put some through a meat grinder and made shit noodles.

During the Festival of the Children we parked our Street Show near the grotto of the Virgin Deer, the favorite animal of La Madre de Los Montaños. Many pilgrims came. After they offered their morsels to Raheno the albino rat, they stayed to watch the Shit Swallower.

One afternoon after Carlos had finished a plateful of shit he held up his plate to the audience like an obedient child. "See," he smiled, "I finished every last bit."

A murmur passed through the crowd. Suddenly one of the pilgrims exclaimed, "It's the face of *White Deer*. Look! On the plate! The face of *White Deer!*"

We saw it too. Clearly outlined on the plate was the image of the popular folk Goddess' favorite pet. Two pilgrims were outraged; a small fistfight erupted. But others began tossing coins toward the plate.

"Stop! Stop!" Carlos pleaded. "You'll destroy the image."

He signaled me to catch the coins in my drum. Miguel grabbed the plate and put it to dry in the sun.

"You," he shouted to me. "Keep the flies away!"

Then Carlos stepped up to the crowd. "I'm making a display," he announced. "Give me your testimonials. Witness this miracle."

It only took one day for Carlos to build a display case with the plate and the image, testimonials from the audience, and a diagram authenticating the table, the chair, the section of the city where the miracle occurred and the date and time.

We made good money. For a while he even stopped swallowing shit because so many pilgrims and curiosity seekers dropped by. Not everyone who came believed. Very few, in fact, did.

Many came to get an extra blessing or out of fear of the consequences if they ignored a miracle.

But like all good schemes, this one came to an end, too. In his haste to put the display together, Carlos left gaps in the wooden joints. Ants soon found their way, unnoticed, into the interior and onto the substance on the plate, and then the face of *White Deer* disappeared.

Two
Living or Dead

DUNG EATERS

To visit a friend who lived on a farm in a remote fishing village on the Bay of Bengal in eastern India I took a train to Puri, then walked seven miles east along the beach. His village was located between Puri and Konarak, the site of the famous sun temple in the state of Orissa. I visited another Sun temple once, a continent away near the Nile. The Egyptian temple was a tall monument in stone that rose above the sandy wastelands where there was little to worship, except for the sun, the sand, and perhaps one or two creatures industrious enough to eke out an existence there.

An English Tibetan scholar E. Evans-Wentz once lived on the property near the ocean in Orissa, but his dwelling had disintegrated over the years. The ruins of a decrepit wood and mud meditation retreat added a mysterious quality to the farm. John built a straw and thatch hut on stilts where he lived with his Tibetan wife and two children.

The family grew tapioca and mustard greens. Sewang, John's wife, taught me to forage for wild greens in the jungle. She pulled buckets of water from an outdoor well. When I inquired about the facilities, Sewang pointed in the direction of the sand dunes. Not only was there no plumbing, there wasn't even an outhouse. Villagers used the vast stretch of dunes near the sea as a natural latrine.

Toilets were rare in rural India. I was accustomed to outhouses if available, and if not, then a bush or tree worked, too. In fact the few public toilets I encountered in villages were so wretched, I preferred the natural setting under a cashew nut tree or behind a palm where there was always some industrious creature or odd plant to observe.

On my first morning I wandered off over a distant sand dune; the barren landscape had few weeds or trees. Not long after I arrived at a remote spot sheltered between two sand dunes, two sizable black beetles appeared at the top of the dune and proceeded down the side in my direction. They were enormous, black and ugly. I didn't wait to see if they bit or pinched. Their antennae clicked feverishly; the pinchers were pointy and ominous.

"Don't worry," Sewang told me later. "They don't bite; they're harmless dung beetles."

I stayed with John and Sewang for a month. Every day I made a trip to the sand dunes and every day I encountered two or three of these insects. They relied on wind-borne scents to locate food or dung. Their timing was uncanny to say the least. Creepy was more to the point.

On a typical day, the beetles skimmed across the sand with great agility. Their bodies were large enough to withstand the strong sea winds, but light enough to scurry atop the soft sand. Heavier creatures faced the arduous task of wading through sand, dragging up one foot at a time only to sink back in as the weight shifted forward. With hard shells for armor and pinchers for front legs, the beetles seemed ready for combat. No barefoot villager dared to step on a beetle for fear of getting pinched. Besides, stomping on a beetle would only push its body deeper into the soft, sheltering sand.

The dung beetles, it turned out, were mannerly. They did not devour dung with a fiendish gluttony. A beetle did not even conspicuously nibble at a dung heap. Rather the black feelers tapped at a mound as if to test consistency and quality. Sometimes a beetle circled a pile to make some further determinations before gingerly separating a hunk from the mass. The beetle then proceeded to shove the chunk, turning it over and over, rounding the mass into a ball with each step forward. The ball gathered a fine coating of sand as the beetle marched off, clearly at ease with maneuvering a piece twice his body size, maintaining control of it up and down the dune.

Not content with a single ball, a beetle scurried back, often accompanied by another beetle. They did not growl or hiss at each other, to claim ownership. They worked together diligently like worker ants until the entire dung pile was carted off, destined for some sandy tunnel, perhaps, where the dung beetles lived and stored the dung balls as a hedge against a season of famine. The entire process was very tidy; the sand coating effectively dulled any stench and the perpetual movement kept the flies away.

It's easy to attribute positive qualities to these scavengers. They're ecologically useful. By eliminating dung, they also eliminate a major food source for disease-carrying maggots. The ritual repeats regularly; beetles scurry away day after day with fresh excrement and the dunes outside of the village are swept clean.

Judging by their external appearance, the black beetles seemed destined for longevity; their hard shells appeared indestructible to natural predators. Indeed, the black armor looked unappetizing. The beetles were also industrious, hardy and patient. To subsist in a harsh desert was not easy. By surviving and flourishing, the beetle achieved a type of immortality.

The ancient Egyptians worshipped the dung-eating scarab. They associated its periodic, temporary descent into the underworld as a sign of everlasting life. The scarab was, in fact, a member of the same scarabaeid family that included the Indian dung beetle. Scarabs were chiseled into stone on ancient sarcophagi, featured in frescos in underground tombs. Amulets were cast in gold and inlaid with turquoise and coral stones. The image of the scarab is still omnipresent in Egypt; replicas of ancient stone carvings are molded in cheap clay and sold as souvenirs to tourists.

I never saw a live scarab in Egypt. I remember my visit to the temple of Karnak near the Nile where I saw many hieroglyphics and where I even bought a cheap, imitation necklace of turquoise clay scarabs. The Indian sun temple of Konarak on the Bay of Bengal was at the same latitude as the ancient Egyptian temple at Karnak. The proximity of the temples to great bodies of water seemed more than a coincidence. Not only that, Konarak and Karnak sound phonetically related.

Did ancient sea-going vessels ply the waters between the two continents? Maybe the scarabs were trapped and exported as temple charms. Or did they stow away in the hold? The physical alignment of both temples also coincides with certain positions of the sun. Only one day a year, on the morning of the day of the summer solstice rays of the sun penetrate a specially carved window in the Konarak temple so the sun lights up the shrine of Surya, Hindu god of the sun, in the innermost sanctum.

I wondered what the English scholar and translator of Buddhist texts from the Tibetan thought of the dung beetles when he walked across these dunes fifty years before me? Between translating passages from the *Tibetan Book of the*

Dead that depicted the lonely transmigration of the Tibetan soul, did he look up and speculate on the nature of the dung beetle? If so, was he reminded, as I am, of the sacred scarab, purveyor of an Egyptian immortality? The ancient Egyptians wrote their own book of the dead and the English translator mentioned the ancient mysteries of Egypt in his preface to the Tibetan book.

Surely the Egyptian scarab, keeper of the human soul, was worshipped for a similar diligence. The scarab plied a desert or similar hostile environment to retrieve a rare essence not to be consumed but to be stored. With unfaltering zeal perhaps, the scarab, armored and treacherous steadfastly transported the dung, like a human soul, safeguarded between black pinchers, to some subterranean tunnel.

Later beneath the desert floor the dung larvae hatched from the inert and detestable mass. Was this regeneration the sign that linked the scarab, in the Egyptian myth, with the emergence of the soul after death?

Was that how these insects came to be worshipped—for their meticulous character, mannerly habits of hard work, and ability to regenerate in a dark, barren subterranean place—and not judged by the foul nature of their diet?

Who could have guessed that the lowly creatures of the dung heaps reaped such honor in the hierarchy of the rich Egyptian pantheon of divine beings. Who could have guessed that such implausible creatures once adorned the necks of beautiful princesses in ancient Egypt.

LEECH HALL OF FAME

Not far from the base of the world's highest glaciers in the Himalayas, the terrain is dense with tropical banana trees and century plants. When I trekked out of Darjeeling and crossed the Indian border into Nepal, incredibly leeches thrived in the moist meadows of snow melt at 7,000 feet. Leeches lived in the grasses and ground cover and sometimes dropped from overhead branches.

I first saw leeches in a movie: I think it was "The African Queen." The leeches were a sinister waterborne menace. The actors pulled the bloodsuckers off their skin carefully to avoid hemorrhaging.

Pioneer American doctors carried jars of leeches to apply to patients' skin as a blood-letting remedy. "At the first sign of inflammation," an old medical text suggested, "apply leeches in good numbers equally distanced from one another."

When I walked in leech country, I worried about my most vulnerable area, only a part of which I could see. To pee outdoors, I squatted perilously close to the grass where the leeches abounded. What if a leech attached itself to a sensitive spot, and bored into a deep place I couldn't see?

And what about menstrual blood? A leech affixed in the appropriate cavity in a woman's body might even be useful when the flow is heavy. And it's possible the gentle, consistent sucking of a leech might even be pleasurable depending on the area of attachment.

When I walked in leech country, every tickle or twitch was cause for concern. I scanned the surface of my skin each night for black bumps. Where I couldn't see, I felt for suspicious knobs. I inspected every crevice before I slept: under my chin and arms, behind my ears and knees, between my toes. I didn't want to wake up and find a gluttonous leech attached to my flesh.

Walking in leech country was spooky. The constant menace lurked in the back of my mind. The parasites conjured up the voracious hungry ghosts who, because of bad karma, were reborn into one of the hellish Buddhist realms where they suffered constant thirst or hunger. Nothing these hungry ghosts or *pretas* drank could assuage the continual fire that raged in their stomachs. Their gullets were so small they couldn't swallow enough food or drink to appease the fierce gnawing within.

Leech sightings were common in the mountains. A pilgrim told me about a mother whose baby howled so loudly no one could sleep. When she went to see why the child was so upset, the mother found a leech firmly attached to one of the baby's eyes. The leech had expanded from the size of a chick pea to the length and thickness of the mother's thumb. The baby never regained sight in the eye that was sucked clean by a leech.

I heard another leech story from a Peace Corps volunteer stationed near Mt. Everest. For weeks he suffered from piercing headaches and a bloody nose. He consulted an *ayurvedic* doctor who gave him a medicine but it had no effect. The headaches continued. One day at a village chai shop as the man blew his nose into a handkerchief a friend just happened to spot the tail end of a black blob disappear up a nostril.

"Ew. You've got a black bug in your nose. Blow hard," he

urged. "Maybe you can blow it out."

The man blew as hard as he could but whatever his friend saw had disappeared. Word spread around the village about the man with the nose bleeds. A group of elders gathered at the chai shop one morning. A village doctor armed with a pair of tweezers and a skill only he possessed managed to extricate a glistening black leech from the depths of the man's nostrils.

The squirming leech was not only ugly but it was the largest one ever seen. On the advice of a friend in the village, the man deposited the creature in a jar filled with formaldehyde. The speimen was packaged carefully to survive the long journey over land and sea all the way to the Smithsonian Museum where it has resided ever since. The man's headaches and nosebleeds continued for a day, then cleared up.

Flesh or Blood

In one of the Jataka tales, the Buddha was born as a tigress in an early incarnation. During meager times, the tigress was unable to find sufficient food for her two cubs, so in a supreme gesture of compassion, the tigress gave up her body to nourish her offspring. I visited the site on the outskirts of Kathmandu where this sacrifice took place. Only a few trees and a shrine marked the spot the Nepalese and Tibetans call *Stamo Lujin*, the place where "the tigress offered her body."

That historic sacrifice must have set a precedent. Buddhists have long considered gifts of flesh—whether the flesh was consumed or not— as noble offerings. A finger, for instance, might be an honorable sacrifice. It was not uncommon to see a traveling monk missing a finger. I wondered if in the grand scheme of divine retributions, the karmic rewards for such an extreme offering might be greater than an ordinary offering of, say, money, incense or fruit?

Buddhist scriptures advise people to never kill any living creature. Would a compassionate Buddhist extend that philosophy to include offering assistance to any creature? Would a Buddhist consider intentionally nourishing a parasite like a leech? A Buddhist would never kill a leech, but could the sacrifice of a few ounces of blood from an extended arm be construed as a good deed or meritorious act?

A monk told me his solution for head lice if he captured any: put them on a pat of butter inside a folded piece of paper where the lice can live out their lives. No need to kill the critters.

On my trek through the land of the leeches, I watched

out for those who were lucky enough, in spite of my sharp surveillance, to find a patch of skin and gently bore in, mingling our bloods.

If I found one soon after attaching to my skin, the leech was easy to disengage. When a leech went undetected for a time, the body puffed up and was harder to pull off. If I forcefully yanked a bloated leech off my skin, the gaping wound might bleed profusely or hemorrhage.

On one occasion a leech became so large, I was afraid to pull it off. What if some of the body remained behind? Or was I confusing a leech with some other parasite like a tick or a chigger?

I poked gently at first around the area of attachment to loosen the suction. Soon my annoyance kicked in: "Let go, damnit! Get the fuck off!"

The leech loosened. I flicked it off my skin. The wound bled. The leech, about the thickness of a pencil, rolled to the ground.

Another monk let a mosquito siphon blood as a type of offering. Would his karmic rewards be greater if he fed a larger insect such as a leech rather than a tiny mosquito? Or was the thought behind the gift what was most important?

I envisioned meeting Yama, the Black Lord of death as he held up his metal balance scales in the *bardo,* the intermediate state after death and before rebirth. As the departed souls lined up for their reckoning: white stones weighed in the good deeds, black stones weighed in the bad.

"Here's a white stone," Yama might say when he sees me standing there, "for the time you fed the leech..."

"But Yama, that was an accident. I didn't want a leech boring into my skin."

On the other hand why rush to judgement? The leech might be an incarnation of the Buddha or some other saint in disguise. If that was the case maybe I'll reap some karmic reward like a trip to a Buddhist heaven, or a spot in the lucky hereafter.

River View

Our summer retreat one year was a house in Kulu—that Kumaon valley paradise of glacier-fed rivers, mountain trout, alpine wildflower honey and steamy hot springs bubbling out of the earth in the foothills of the western Himalayas. Graham and I rented a newly built house close to the river on the outskirts of a village. Graham claimed an upstairs room off a small balcony for his studio that overlooked woods behind the bungalow. A large picture window offered a view of the river. Behind us village houses rose like stepping stones up the mountain.

A boy brought water in two brass pots suspended by ropes from a yoke over his shoulders. That saved me from standing in line at the village faucet. I practiced Tibetan calligraphy with a handcarved bamboo pen I dipped into a small clay bowl filled with jet black sumi ink. To bake a loaf of bread I placed the dough in a small tin that fit inside an empty larger pot perched camping style over the single-burner kerosene stove. Graham strummed the strings of a sitar he bought and studied Indian classical music. At night we read by the light of a kerosene lantern.

The village women wore deep maroon velvet jackets covered with dozens of round mirrors embroidered directly onto the fabric. When I found some loose mica on a nearby path I decided to try my hand at embroidery—about which I knew absolutely nothing.

To begin I threaded a needle from my sewing kit. Not knowing any embroidery stitches, I sewed the flat mirror-like jagged flat stones onto a piece of cotton cloth with a cobweb effect. Stitches zigzaged around each little disk, securing it in place.

Two weeks after we moved in men from the village dragged a cow carcass to the huge boulder in front of our bungalow. The rock was flat like a platform.

"Look what's in our front yard!" I said.

"What?" Graham looked up from re-stringing his sitar.

"A dead cow—check it out."

"Say what?"

The next day swarms of flies traipsed across the body. We could hear the buzzing through closed windows.

A stench wafted in the breeze. High overhead a few vultures circled the site before swooping down. Two landed directly on top of the carcass. More birds joined in. Squabbles and claw fights broke out. Newcomers shoved their way into the crowd standing atop the bloated carcass like a crowd milling around an accident site. One beaked out the eyeballs; others ripped into the stomach, played tug of war over glistening strings of intestines.

As the vultures picked apart the corpse and gorged on carrion, I felt as if I was sitting in a front row seat at a freak show where each gross act upstaged the last one. Our river view turned omnious before our very eyes. To think our little cottage now bordered a rural animal cemetery. Instead of prime river front property, we lived above an open air burial ground. No wonder the village houses rose *up* the hill.

"What now?" I moaned.

"Shut the window tight!"

"It's tight!"

"Put up a drape or something. That might help."

For a day the birds gorged themselves, flinging pieces of

bloody meat around. They stopped jabbing beaks and ripping claws into each other and defended prime eating spots. Once they feasted the ruckus quieted down. Stately, immobile birds stood around like morners at a burial.

"They ate. What's keeping them here? Why don't they leave?"

"They're full."

"So—"

"Too full to fly!"

"What do you mean?"

"It's a party. They're hung over waiting to digest their food."

"Oh, God. How long will that take?"

Death and corpses trotted in and out of my dreams. In the morning I drank my usual pot of brewed Darjeeling tea at my seat by the picture window. The gritty, ragged scavengers slept standing up, huddled shoulder to shoulder atop the boulder. They looked like grim undertakers in black tuxedos.

We shouted, clapped as loud as we could, stomped and grunted like maniacs to try and scare the birds away. Not a single one twitched or moved a muscle. This was their party. We were the interlopers.

"Look at it this way: vultures are carnivores but they're not killers." Under pressure Graham maintains equanimity better than I do. His is the voice of reason.

"They're not thieves, either. They're scavengers. The sooner they clean the bones, the quicker they rid the village of maggots."

"What about us? What do we do?"

"Sit somewhere else. Don't look. Meditate on impermanence or something."

"Incorporate rotting flesh into my tantric meditation. Is that it?" I lit a fresh incense stick then checked the window for the umpteenth time to see that it was tightly shut.

"You got it. We'll die sometime. Might as well get used to the idea."

DROUGHT

Raju who lived uphill from our bungalow on the river constantly complained about the weather. "Where is the rain? Why is monsoon is late? Crops are dying. The grass is dead already."

The worst drought in years turned a fertile river valley into a dust bowl. Raju's mule had a harder and harder time locating grass and odd leaves. Hours of grazing turned up only a mouthful of twigs.

With no grass to eat, mule developed a taste for odd foods. Raju did his best to save the outer cabbage leaves, carrot tops, and discarded potato skins, but, lacking these, the colorful comic strip page of the Sunday newspaper was second best. Mule chomped contentedly on the green Sports page and pink Financial sections of the *Hindustan Times*.

Water was rationed and faucets turned on once a day. Village wells ran dry. Down river the water level sank so low it unveiled an entire temple compound sunken many years ago. When heads from two Durga statues appeared in in the mud, a ceremony was initiated by the local pundit who feared the wrath of the goddess was responsible for the lack of rain.

After Raju's water buffalo died of starvation, birds of prey spotted the gaunt carcass in front of our house. Vultures first, then crows squeezed in to peck at the meat.

One young vulture performed a crazy victory dance stepping from one clawed foot to the other, fully extending his five foot wingspan atop the crowded perch. Some birds vomited undigested carrion.

Raju shook his head in disgust. "Life is cruel. It's not fair. My buffalo dies of starvation. These bastards thrive and multiply."

ISLAND OF DEAD ANTS

Graham spotted a bargain at the weekly open air market—a jumbo hummingbird feeder for three rupees. The feeder was priced right but I was leery of street vendor gadgets with one exception—outsider artists' handmade whirli-gig contraptions made from recycled pop cans and chewing gum wrappers. Just because something was fetchingly displayed on a blanket at a flea market didn't mean it was any good.

A small plastic feeder already hung down from the deck. Dainty hummingbirds were a welcome distraction from the vulture melee in the front yard.

Graham mixed coconut milk with sugar to test the new feeder. "It doesn't leak," he announced after viewing the swinging globe for a few minutes.

The enterprising hummingbird that first scoped out the giant communal feeder was an aggressive maniac. He exhausted himself chasing interlopers away. Since there was a constant stream of thirsty, sugar-lusting birds, he kept busy from dawn to dusk. The territorial hummingbird and a host of speedy trespassers busily guzzled and flew off like commuter coffee addicts getting their fix at a drive-up take-out window.

A nice thing about the jumbo feeder with the built-in perches was the potential to view birds up close as they tippled. This one had platforms, enough room for six hummingbirds to sit down, take a breather, and contentedly guzzle the sugary brew mixed up in the kitchen.

The cheap feeder took our minds off the vulture fracas

until a puddle underneath the feeder attracted a dozen large red ants I hadn't seen before. The ants burrowed a tunnel under the leaky feeder and surrounded the puddle of ambrosic *amrita* that trickled down from the swinging red sky globe above their heads.

Lazy ants sucked the sweetened mud while curious ones set out to discover the source of a new elixir. Were they lured by the sweet scent or could they see with their minuscule eyes so close to the ground that a feeder dangled from the tree branch? In no time contingents of ants trekked up the trunk of the pine tree by the side of the house and trailed out the limb to personally assess the guzzling potential of the feeder.

Raju stopped by. We agreed small birds were easier to watch than the oversized outcastes that plundered the carcass in the front yard. He didn't share our enthusiasm nor our amusement over the feeder. The price of sugar or the waste of sugar on wild birds bothered him. He never understood why we traveled to his small village in the first place. What was the attraction?

Hell if we knew. But being there was carthartic and restful. Every time I walked by the feeder I monitored the ants' progress at the puddle and on the overhead branch. Noses twitched as ants inspected the swinging glass up close. Tiny feelers waved frantically as ants descended into the spouts the birds were supposed to guzzle from. Minutes later ants reappeared treading wildly in the thick soup inside the feeder.

"They got in. I warned you about cheap products."

"Did you know ants could swim?" Graham deadpanned. He had a vested interest in the success of the hummingbird feeder since he was the one who bought it.

"They tread water, but for how long?"

The feeders were transparent so every movement inside was clearly visible. Unlike bathers at the Great Salt Lake whose bodies easily floated in salt-thickened water, these ants weren't floaters in a thick sugar bath. They thrashed around, splayed in the syrup until they exhausted themselves and drowned. Limp belly-up bodies crowded the surface.

One ant clung to a dead ant to stay afloat. Somehow the dead ones bunched up in the middle of the jumbo sugar lake until a black mound of roughly twenty bodies floated like a self-contained island, an island of dead ants. Newcomer ants crawled up on top of the mass grateful for a place to take a breather.

The island of bodies grew overnight. The next day more ants jumped, fell, or squeezed in. Graham threatened to empty the feeder and start over. Who could blame him? No self-respecting hummingbird wanted to drink elixir littered with dead comrades. When Graham completed his self-appointed task, the last remnant of the island of dead ants that we'd been charting for days vanished like a genie in an old science fiction movie.

BALCONY

When I met Graham at an artist Open Studio tour his large canvases filled the walls of his cluttered basement studio in the flatlands of Emeryville. In Kulu he paints on a portable canvas pad. His charcoal drawings of the Rhotang pass were small but he planned to expand them into paintings when we returned.

Yesterday flies drew his attention to the balcony above the back deck. Flies surrounded an unidentified brown mound buried in wild mulberry leaves.

"What the hell? Who crapped on the balcony?"

Graham wasn't the culprit. He would never shit on his own doorstep and by extension his balcony. Wasn't that something his mother once said? Graham worked in solitude. We entertained no visitors. Nor did we have a dog. What's more, the offender didn't enter the balcony through the inside door. That was always locked. Whatever intruded came from outside.

Who or what would climb a tree to crap on a balcony? On closer inspection the pile wasn't an isolated occurrence. Five distinct heaps were scattered in the leaves. The question then became: why climb a tree on private property to crap on a balcony not once but as many as five times?

Graham inspected the piles. They appeared animal in nature. At least no human trespasser fouled his balcony. Still animal bodily fluids and droppings were problematic. Insects and wild animals can spread diseases. Saliva from a rabid animal posed a health threat. Didn't mice feces spread the plague or legionaire's disease or both?

Plastic gloves weren't sold in the village market so Graham put his hand inside a plastic bag to pick up the crap.

If we were home or within walking distance of an internet cafe he'd research animal tracks in the dirt out back or wild scat specimens.

"Fox or skunk," Raju said on his way to the market."They're common near the village. Skunk. Foxes don't climb. Must be a skunk."

"Why would a skunk," Graham asked after Raju left, "go to the trouble of climbing a tree to crap on the balcony?"

"At least it didn't stink up the place," I said.

To get to the bottom of this involved some convoluted thinking—something Graham was good at.

"If someone needed to crap outdoors he or she would pick an isolated spot not near a building."

"Yeah."

"Behind a bush or in the woods. Bushes provide privacy."

"OK." I wasn't sure where he was headed with this.

"A wild spot worked best because a natural area was not landscaped. There would be no question of trespassing or fouling private property."

"O.K."

"The wilder the area the better to crap unnoticed."

"And dig a hole so you don't leave any evidence behind."

"To a skunk who roamed up and down a river bank thick with pine, mulberry and oak the entire natural habitat was part of the natural living space. In other words if an animal kept house in the woods, the woods were it's living quarters."

"Yeah."

"If a skunk wanted to relieve himself in a spot that was away from his natural lair and not part of the common dwelling area, then the "unnatural" place to go would be in the vicinity of a manmade building. Especially a newly built building."

Buildings weren't natural structures. I agreed with that. Our building could be in the way, an obstacle for a skunk who roamed the untamed regions surrounding this Himalayan village on the banks of a trout stream.

"Buildings are the transgressors, the bane of wilderness areas, the source, the progenitor of stinky, noisy, toxic, congested activity. The balcony with it's layer of dried up leaves is right smack in the middle of an invasive manmade building which rises in all it's ugliness at the edge of the woods.

"To a skunk a reasonable place to crap might be directly on this offending building that protrudes above the hallowed forest floor. No skunk habitat is spoiled in the process. And if there is an element of protest inherent in this contentious or conscientious act, so much the better."

Not to be out-smarted by a tree climbing skunk intent on taking a crap, Graham stood on the balcony to defiantly mark territory. He pissed into the wind spraying the tree trunk and saturating the bark.

Once the skunk started to climb the urine-drenched tree one whiff would alert him to danger. Any culprit who dared trespass here could arouse the ire of a foul smelling tree-pisser.

THREE
THE RAT CHRONICLES

THE RAT QUEEN

In a colony of East African mole rats the Queen rules. She is larger than the others and holds court in the roomiest chamber of the warren. There are other females but they are not fertile. The Queen is the only rat with swollen nipples.

When the Queen moves through the twisting underground tunnels of the colony, the others prostrate before her. Each rat performs this underground protocol; there are no abstainers and no questions are asked. As the Queen steps over the prostrate bodies she learns the state of her charges; their feet reek of the garbage dumps, toilet pits, and funeral grounds, places they've tramped in their nocturnal expeditions. By the scent on the feet of the hairless mole rats a Queen predicts abundance or depravity in the upper ground world outside the colony.

Female rats touch noses with their Queen when she passes. Nose to nose, they kiss in this way, not by choice but by decree. When a rat's nose touches the nose of the Queen, hidden messages are spoken in an inaudible tongue. A touch, a caress, the scent of each female speaks of her desire, her condition, her heretical dream, perhaps, to propagate and nurture, to give birth to her own tiny hairless baby mole rats, to ascend to the role of Queen mother.

The Queen will not tolerate the fertility of others. When females greet her and brush noses in their daily obeisance, she offers, in return, the kiss of sterility, a kiss of death. The Queen sweats a lethal perfume that inhibits other females, numbs their sexual desire and stops the growth of the organs of their sex. With no drive and no organs, the females do not conceive and reproduce. A Queen rules in this way for many seasons, many litters.

If a female holds out and abstains from the deadly kiss, she may develop breasts and swollen nipples. When this happens the Queen acts quickly and kills the upstart who flaunts sexuality, an ability to procreate.

When a Queen dies or leaves the colony, chaos ensues. The turmoil that supplants an orderly society of mole rats is a condition that develops in other colonies, too. Kingdoms of ants or people on every continent lose rulers. Sometimes the transition to establish a new leader is smooth. More often contenders battle until only one survives.

Reincarnation

In the colony of mole rats there is no line of succession. Since all offspring are children of the former Queen, there is no single heir to the throne. After a Queen's demise a few females develop sexual organs. Swollen nipples appear on their chests and sexual instincts, no longer dormant, are aroused. Clashes follow. The females fight each other for the privilege or duty of ruling the colony. Only one Queen can dominate so the females fight until one gains supremacy.

The males keep their distance until the battles are over. They wait for the victorious Queen to summon them into her chamber. Mature males do little besides breed; it is the job they do best. Young workers are left to journey alone or in pairs outside to gather food. The young also work hard to keep the tunnels and chambers of the colony clean.

When a Queen dies the mole rats do not labor over stone monuments to erect in her honor. They do not bury her with her favorite rice gruel and sugar millet cakes. Workers drag her body to the end of an abandoned tunnel in the underground colony, then fill the entrance with dirt.

The dead Queen rests in state for the time it takes for her body to degenerate. When the worms and grubs that bore into her plump flesh, bore out again into tunnels of their own making and into lives quite different from those of the mole rats in the underground colony, her reincarnation will be complete.

Rat Tavern

The rats did not build the tavern nor do they stock the bar but rats are the only customers in one underground watering hole. When the tavern opened rats knew nothing about bars, lounges or taverns but very quickly they wandered the underground corridors in the sunless expanse like tourists on a Caribbean holiday and soon discovered a bar in a central area.

Only the rats that lived in the colony under glass were able to imbibe at the tavern since all passageways to the outside world were securely sealed. A rat needed no money to gain entrance; no bouncers guarded the door. There were no barstools or pool tables, no glasses or beer mugs but the rats had an unlimited supply of alcohol.

Thirsty rats chose their drinks. At the bar three spouts dispensed water from inverted glass bottles and three dispensed an anise flavored liqueur that tasted like Greek *ouzo*. All residents had an equal chance to patronize the tavern. They dropped in at any time night or day and drank their beverage of choice.

In the colony there were areas where rats ate, slept, and played. Drinking wasn't the only activity available. Like other booze drinkers, the alcoholic rats developed habits: they drank two hours before dinner at gregarious cocktail-like gatherings and they took nips before bed. Every three to four days the heavier drinkers binged and drank themselves silly.

When an intoxicated rat dozed off in the middle of a main thoroughfare in an underground tunnel, a team of rats dragged the comatose drunkard into an adjoining chamber by biting into his tail and pulling. There on his back with his four paws suspended, gently churning the air in the groggy slumber of inebriates, the unconscious rat slept off his stupor.

For seven years the rat tavern dispensed beverages on demand to any resident of the rat colony. Each year the alcoholic rats became more set in their ways: they drank after they woke up, had another drink before lunch, two at dinner and one before bed. The drunks did not sleep well at night, were lethargic during the day, and developed liver and brain damage.

In the eighth year of operation the tavern closed. Nondrinkers found quarters in another colony under glass. A few rats moved to private cages where they were tempted with other spiked beverages and gruel.

When the alcohol disappeared the drinkers grew irritable. Some died in rat fights; others became malnourished. Males lacked the desire to procreate so no baby rats were born. Before a year was over, the last remaining rat which frequented the rat tavern died so no one was left to tell the younger rats—if any ever showed up—of the proverbial fountain of limitless drink in the underground tavern of rats.

THE QUOTA

Indonesian farmers measure their wealth by the towers of rice in the storage bins. For a time every fall the rice harvests are plentiful. One year the winter was long and the grain disappeared faster than usual. By February village elders feared the food would not last through the summer.

As the villagers worried, the rats feasted. There was plenty of rice for them. No need to hoard and store. With an abundance of food and a high fertility rate, the rat population swelled. Rats easily slipped through knotholes in the wooden silo bins, scaled walls, and dug tunnels. There was hardly a rice bin that wasn't impenetrable by a gnawing rat.

Even though there was food, the rats knew they were not welcomed to it. Stealth and speed were skills they used to outrun rocks hurled at them. If a rat strayed too close to the village, an angry housewife chased after him, swinging a broomstick or frying pan.

Fearing the predicted shortage of grain, the government moved to address the swelling rodent population. An order was issued: farmers, young men, boys, students, housewives, girls and anyone who could walk must mobilize efforts to reduce the rat population. Furthermore, no kerosene or sugar would be sold in the village until a minimum of six hundred rats were killed each day.

At dusk, even though the villagers were tired from working the fields all day, they mustered the energy to mobilize and fulfill their daily quota. Standing three feet apart, the men, women, and children entirely surrounded a section of an infested field. Some carried torches, others wooden clubs.

When the leader signaled "Go!" villagers stomped the ground, cursed and shouted as they moved slowly towards the center, narrowing the circle. The torchbearers shoved flaming sticks into the underground nest to drive the rodents out into the open. Women quickly closed in the circle. Then the slaughter began.

A leader tallied the death toll. Often he reached six hundred bodies and still the pile in each field stood taller than a ladder, taller than two men standing end to end but not as tall as the coconut palm which grew at the edge of the village.

Rat Tax

Cuando suena con un raton, se va a casar uno de la familia.
When you dream of a rat, someone in the family will get married.

In an adjacent Indonesian village the chief ordered villagers to pay a rat tax. Owners of rice hullers were the hardest hit by the tax. Since they stored large quantities of grain, their shops were popular with the rat thieves. Each season the hullers paid one hundred rats to stay in business.

Before a marriage could be consecrated or a divorce granted the prospective couples from the village must pay the special rat tax: it costs ten rats to get married and twenty rats to get divorced.

"There are no exceptions and no one is allowed to buy the rats or employ others to catch them," the village chief instructed. That is why the day before a marriage ceremony, the parents and grandparents spend the day cooking and cleaning while the bride-to-be and her young groom dress in old clothes, leave home early, and hunt for rats to trap and kill to pay the rat tax so the priest can join them in matrimony.

WHARF RATS

Down at the harbor where the breakwater meets the wharf rats hover in the crevices between the kelp strewn rocks. They nest on the harbor side, out of the way of the sloshing sea breakers. To supplement a diet of dead gulls, cod, herring, sewage and garbage, rats catch shellfish.

A rat's tail is multifunctional. A musical rat thumps out rhythms with his tail, pounds out a steady beat as other rats improvise night music: moonlight barn sonatas, thundering harbor blues, melancholy warehouse tunes. With a tail held up or down, a rat engineer measures the height of passageways, the depths of sinkholes. A blind rat bites into a fellow rat's tail then follows his lead through an unknown passage.

Harbor crabs live in the same rocky sea wall as the harbor rats only the crabs dwell underwater. To fish a rat balances on a rocky overhang, dangles his tail at least three inches into the water, then wiggles provocatively.

Is that a twig, a piece of rope or a seaweed tube? A crab might wonder.

Patience is an integral part of fishing—patience to sit and wait for a bite. As soon as a crab grabs the rat's tail it maneuvers the spindled thing into its mouth for an exploratory taste. Immediately the rat flips his tail straight up out of the water flinging the astonished crab—still clinging to the tail—on shore.

On land a crab is no match for a rat. In an instant a rat chews off the crab's legs, disabling the creature, then leisurely cracks apart the shell piece by piece to nibble the tender meat. The curious crab that grasps after an eel-like worm jutting into the water from an undetermined source on the rocks above his head is the one at risk of being flung ashore by a harbor rat.

Since there are enough fish carcasses that sink to the sea bottom to feed legions of crabs, wise crabs should keep their sights limited to a few feet in front of them to avoid whatever distractions the upper waters tempt.

Rat Fishing in Ohio

In one Ohio tournament people bait the hooks on their fishing poles with pieces of Stilton or Tillamook cheese, cold hot dogs, raw steak or bacon, then toss their lines out at night. They don't fish for trout or shad at the river's edge or in the lakes and ponds of forest preserves nor do they sit patiently in rowboats as their lines slice pathways through choppy lake waters.

The people cast their lines into the back alleys of a few large cities where garbage festers with maggots and bacteria. Bets are wagered on who will snag the largest rat.

The fishermen do not fish for rats to grill on the barbecue. No juicy pieces of blackened grilled rat fillets rest atop beds of sliced lettuce and watercress on serving platters in the backyards of Dayton or Toledo.

"Rat fishing is a big sport around here," a Middletown barkeep explains. "Guys fish for rats at our annual contest. This is not a fraternity stunt. Winning takes skill. The man who hooks the largest rat wins.

"Contestants abide by the rules. No artificial lures, trotlines, bells, whistles or firearms allowed. No rat padding or stuffing—that last rule originated after one man, lacking a modicum of good sportsmanship, rammed a lead weight down a rat's throat to increase the weight. No, sir. That's verbotten.

"We give prizes for the largest rat caught and for the largest number of rats caught from midnight until 2:00 a.m."

Although prime rat feeding time is midnight to 2:00 a.m., during the contest rats change their habits to avoid crowds of men who light cigarettes, spit, cuss, and howl with drunken glee as they bait their hooks.

Rats aren't stupid. They keep to themselves mostly, avoid noisy commotions.

"The first spring a fisherman's wife snagged a rat with a hook baited with Hormel's smoked bacon fat. She reeled fast and hard. On a meat scale the barkeep weighed the specimen in a clear plastic bag. The couple won first place with their prize catch: a twelve and a half-inch one pounder."

Like any sport or political contest, rat fishing has its detractors. One reporter with ties to city hall blames the contest for attracting rats, rather than deterring nocturnal scavengers from prowling the city's alleys. Politicians take sides: they can cast votes to either keep the tradition of rat fishing alive or to scrap the contest altogether.

"Maybe our contest attracts a rat or two," the barkeep speaks up in defense of his contest, "but I doubt it. Anyone taken a rat census lately? Check the figures. There are more rats than people in some areas. Truth is, rats are here whether we entice them out of their holes or not. Count 'em. Those guys in city hall aren't addressing the problem. The purpose of our contest is to draw attention to the problem. We not only succeed, we have a good time."

CROCODILE'S BAIT

In Florida's gater-infested swamps, crocodiles fish, too. They bait their jaws to lure their prey. Unlike the rats, those agile land creatures that supplement their diets with shellfish, crocodiles come ashore to whet their appetites with land critters.

Before a crocodile restes his enormous head on the banks of a swampy river that meanders through a city, he carefully leaves a tidbit of food resting on his immobile tongue or wedged between long pointy teeth. The crocodile without so much as a flicker of an eyelid or a barely audible snort, waits with opened jaws for an unsuspecting creature to come and sniff the bait.

With luck a rat may amble by and catch a whiff of a scavenged waterlogged cheese sandwich or a hamburger scrap. The crocodile must lay perfectly still, absolutely immobile to gain a rat's trust. No sneezing or gurgling when delicate rat feet traipse over his watering tongue as the rat creeps closer to inspect the smelly saliva-coated mouth.

One footstep follows another in rapid succession. The rat's nose stretches ahead. The jaws of death hover with anticipation then suddenly clamp shut with a quick, irreversible—Whoomp!

TEMPLE RATS

Over the centuries oriental rats earned the respect of philosophers and artists. The Chinese named calligraphy brush strokes after rats. Artists claimed the way trifoliated leaves spread out from the branches of a tree resembled *rat footprints*. Rats became associated with the enlightened master's holy robe. That is, the cloth that drapes over the body of a meditating Buddha statue was said to bunch like *a rat's tail*.

In one Japanese tale a young novice monk's hands were tied behind his back after he was caught drawing instead of reciting prayers in the temple with the other monks. Even though his hands were tightly bound, his big toe etched the outline of three sharp-toothed rats in the dust. The rodents were so realistic they sprang to life, gnawed the ropes and freed the tethered monk.

In another myth a Japanese traveler accidentally fell down a tunnel that led to a secret underworld abode where industrious four-footed rodents harvested, bound and rolled large rice bales for winter food storage. He watched a rat overseer keep tally on his abacus. Other rats weighed gold coins and made enormous rice cakes. There was never a quiet moment.

The rodents were as compatible and hard-working as ants; everyone busy from dawn to dusk. The ambiance of the sprawling underground haven so enthralled the traveller, he was reluctant to leave. He can still be found, in fact, in temple paintings and woodblock prints in ancient books, hiding behind an enormous rock spying on the proud, busy and unsuspecting rat farm workers.

Morsels for the Rat Gods

In West Bengal a rat haven, a type of underground heaven that caters to wild rats, is located in a corner of the Central Park in Kolkata near the business district. There is no sign to guide the curious to the underground warren. No tourist maps mark the spot. A visitor might even pass by the busy rat abode without recognizing it.

Just a hop from a busy street where busses, rickshaws, trucks, bullock carts, taxis, and bicycles clamor for the right of way, rats that are fortunate to have found this spot, freely circle in burrowed tunnels in the dry grass.

Food is plentiful. Vendors stand nearby ready to sell dried grains and peanuts, roasted corn kernels and chickpeas, sumptuous morsels fit for a rat king. The vendors' large woven straw trays balance on wobbly makeshift rattan pedestals that are lightweight and easy to pick up after a day's work when they head for the shanties they call home.

Children and adults take turns buying packets of food. One vendor with the confidence of a pizza chef throwing dough into the air, tosses the kernels above his head then catches them in a paper cone he quickly fashions out of a sheet of the *Hindustan Times*. A twist at the top and bottom finish the package.

Children throw nuts to the rats just like children in the parks of Europe and America toss out bread crusts to feed ducks in city ponds. One small girl grips her mother's hand and squeals with delight and horror.

The rats adjust to the wild proliferation of grains falling in the proximity of their busy warren. Every day crowds gather outside the colony. Rats swarm out of dozens of tunnels to grope for the proffered food offerings raining down like manna from the sky.

Blinded by the midday sun, they sniff their way to tiny morsels and gobble down the treats before retreating back into the safety and darkness underground.

In a city where thousands of people with barely a crumb to eat live and beg on the pavements of the streets, the rats, detested scavengers and harbingers of ominous plagues of the past, enjoy an abundance of the tastiest morsels at any time night or day.

RAT SOULS

In Rajastan, an arid region in western India, rats are born into a life of leisure and abundance but only if they are born in the rat temple where they are fed and worshipped.

Every day Hindu pilgrims travel to Rajastan to pay homage to Karni Mata, a 15th century miracle worker who temporarily transformed the souls of deceased villagers into rats to protect them from a marauding devil. Pilgrims bring peanuts, puffed rice and sweets to feed the hundreds of rats running freely in the Karni Mata temple.

Devotees nurture the rats because they believe that after death the rats will be reborn as villagers again. Dingy nutmeg tinged rats carry in their innermost being the souls of grandmothers, uncles and village priests.

Wise pilgrims make offerings to the Goddess Karni Mata who is the only one who can reincarnate and transform the rat souls back into villagers again. A pilgrim wouldn't want to encounter the Goddess in the hereafter and have her look the other way.

A Rat Tooth Myth

"When food is scarce, try wood," goes an unspoken rat credo. Termites eat wood; elephants gnaw, crunch tree limbs, branches, leaves. Wood is plentiful and leaves a taste in the mouth, which is better than the void of starvation.

Like cats that have the constant need to sharpen their claws, rats need to file their teeth on wood—not because the teeth turn dull by chewing on cement or bones. Rather rat teeth never stop growing so if a rat doesn't continually sharpen, gnaw and grind the teeth down, they grow out like fangs, eventually interlock and once the lips lock shut the rat starves.

Some parents throw a child's milk tooth near a rat tunnel. They believe when a rat finds and gnaws on the child's tooth, the gap left by the baby tooth in the child's mouth will soon be replaced by a harder, rat-like steel tooth.

Better the teeth than the bones. If a rat's bones continue to grow, rats could reach the size of cats, then dogs, then cows, and elephants. Their appetites could double, triple, and expand a hundred fold. Think of the ugly mutations, the voracious appetites, and the immense traps needed then to keep the rodents under control.

CURRENCY

In a war torn country, in a season of drought or famine, rats multiply. If a farmer reaps bountiful harvests, rats feast and prosper. The unwritten yet much accepted ideology of rats contains a simple premise: where there is food, there are rats.

To the east in a country where millions of people vie for limited supplies of rice and millet to feed their families there is a bounty offered for rat tails. The assumption is: for every rat tail cashed in, there is a rotting rat corpse left behind since rat tails do not fall off and regenerate at will like lizard tails. No granary is free from invasions by hungry rodents so the higher the rat death toll, the higher the levels of grain stored in the granaries to feed the hungry people.

The more rat tails cashed in, the greater the progress in the War On Rats. Farmers earn fifty *paisa*, about four cents, for each tail. For an exchange of twelve rattails, a farmer buys one hundred grams of rice. The rat war is like a contest: besides monetary rewards, there are prizes. The most popular prize, the one that provides a farmer with the incentive to produce dozens of rubbery dead tails, is a toaster oven.

Rats know the scent of their own. In the dumps outside of the villages when survivor rats paw through the refuse looking for food they discover the severed tails and rotting corpses, the proceeds or discards from the annual contest or war. If rats are able to add and multiply they will understand the magnitude of the slaughter, the potential threat, and the grim atmosphere that prevails in a world where there are perpetual wars and heavy casualties.

A Scam

In *la Ciudad* some rats who nest in cardboard boxes eat regularly without having to scout like they used to, scavenge for scraps in the alleys or dumps or under the floors of *cantinas* or *mercados*.

The trapped rats do not know their captors are thieves, but if they did, they would identify with their wily ways. For aren't rats the ultimate thieves? Rats do not grow their food. There are no cultivated rat gardens or rat tended farms, no rat markets or rat pantries. Rats sometimes hunt but mostly they gather what they can steal from barns and silos if they live on farms. City rats must eke out their subsistence on spoiled, discarded food unless they can steal into kitchen cupboards or grocery storerooms under the pale of an outcast moon.

A thief carries his partner with him when he's out on a job. When not in a cardboard box a rat waits long minutes scrunched up in a baggy coat pocket or in a crackly brown paper sack.

On summer days sweltering city air induces residents to throw open the windows of their apartments and roll down the windows of their cars as they ride through the streets of the capital. The thief stakes his position on a street corner where signals alert drivers to: Halt! *Alto!*

From inside the coat pocket a rat hears the whizzing traffic, the occasional car honk and screech of tire brakes. The pocketed rat associates freedom with the sounds of an automobile. Such confidence comes from experience; he has been out on jobs before. The rat doesn't know when he will be released, but he has an idea of where.

The thief scrutinizes cars that stop at a traffic light since he must choose one to hit quickly before the light changes and the car and driver vacate the intersection. The thief prefers an expensive car like a Mercedes or a Jaguar but if the wait is too long a Cadillac or a Chevrolet will also work. An element of chance is always at play.

After the thief selects a car he swipes the windshield with a dirty sponge while beckoning the driver to give him some *pesos* for his trouble. The thief does not clean the glass but soils the windshield with two broad swipes from a grungy sponge.

The irate driver rolls down the car window. "You ruined my clean window, asshole!" he shouts. "Beat it! Scram!"

Just at that moment, before the driver can finish his rebuke, the thief tosses his rat inside. The rat wastes no time inspecting the floor for droppings.

Men are easier targets than women. Both react with astonished fear but it is the men who readily abandon their cars. Women have a greater desire to protect their property and a greater fear of being stranded in a strange section of the city. Women also spend more time in the *cocinas*, the kitchens, and they are more familiar with rat teeth marks, rat droppings, and the furtive rat silhouettes that lurk at the perimeters of light. Thieves prefer cars driven by men.

At the police station officers piece together one man's story. "Suddenly there's this huge, snarling black rat in the car," he pants. "He's ready to jump at my throat any second. I start screaming: *Help me! Help me!*" No one comes. Just as I throw open the car door and leap out, a twelve-year old boy bolts for the driver's seat. In a flash he slams the door shut with a wallop, guns the motor then races down the *camino.* That was thirty minutes ago. Look at my hands. I'm still shaking. That's the last time I saw my car."

When the thief pockets the money from the fast sale of a stolen car, he rewards the rat with food. Partners in crime care for each other's needs.

After one or two cars the thief abandons his scam, especially if the take was good or the police hot on his trail. The freed rat finds himself back on the streets to prowl the alleys once again for edible refuse and scraps of garbage.

A RAT KING

In a colony of mole rats there is no royal family. A solitary Queen, who does not marry, rules alone. In the underground warren no males are honored with a seat upon the royal throne. No King succeeds a Queen.

When the urge to breed manifests, the Queen selects a worker to come into her chamber where he is welcome for the time it takes to mate. No worker rat expects a rise in social status for the duty or pleasure he provides.

In the annals of ratdom there *is* a rat king but it is neither a royal consort nor a throned leader. Likewise a rat king is neither a male rat nor a solitary rat for that matter. Instead a rat king is a term that describes a group of interconnected rats whose rear end tails, irreversibly entwined, converge in a tight knot.

Eight, ten, twelve or more rats huddle in a circle, butt to butt, heads pointing out. The circular configuration is not a voluntary grouping. The circle of rats is a trap from which no rat escapes. Not all of the rats in a rat king see the other's faces, since they're joined behind their backs, tail to tail. No matter how hard a rat pulls away from the center of the rat king, he or she will not slip free. Rats in a rat king are hitched for life to those who share their fate. A few bottled specimens are found in science labs or curio cabinets, those *wunderkabinettes* of the Middle Ages.

A rat king cannot move unless there is a consensus or communal desire to move to spaces wide enough to accommodate this circular group. Most rat kings never venture from the nest, the place of birth and the place of confinement.

One reason this configuration may be called a rat king with the odd allusion to royalty is that members of a rat king can survive only if other rats bring them food. The privilege of having food placed before them is not unlike the privilege a king enjoys. The rats, like sedentary, gluttonous monarchs, grow fat from lack of exercise.

The tails must be knotted after birth. This is an assumption but one that is easier to imagine than the alternative which is a single mother rat produced this convoluted arrangement in the womb and birthed the entangled litter in one operation.

So if the tails are knotted after birth, who knots the tails? After birth does a harassed mother rat knot the tails of her brood together so the blind babies can't stray from the nest and encounter danger while she scouts for food to feed them? Or are the rats victims of a conniving, vengeful rat—a jealous rat sibling who knots tails together to prevent brother and sister rats from finding a secret food source? Perhaps the knotted tails represent a cruel punishment for rival female contenders to the royal rat throne?

Vengeful motives aside, whoever ties the tails together in the first place—as a joke, as part of a game perhaps—may fully intend to untie the tails but either forgot how or ran away and died before completing the extrication.

There is one other possibility. Maybe the rats in a rat king of their own free will join together, faces pointing outward, tails huddled together. Then in a feat of communal cooperation they layer their tails end to end, interlacing to form a platform, or elevated seat or royal litter upon which the reigning Queen can sit. Rats could then parade their leader on a woven rat-tail throne. Only later did this voluntary grouping of tails become unintentionally knotted. The royal appellation, or the reason the configuration is called a rat king, as opposed to a rat throne or a rat litter, may derive from this royal connection.

A frustrated rat locked in this claustrophobic, neurotic group prays for the proverbial farmer's wife or any bounty hunter to come along armed with a sharp carving knife. To a rat trapped in a rat king the pain or consequences of a severed tail are a small price to pay for that sweet dream of freedom.

A Rat Addict

Rats often indulged in fetid or putrid morsels found in dumps or sewers, but the myth that rats eat anything is far from the truth. City rats never consume garbage indiscriminately. Rats are finicky about what goes into their stomachs since they can't vomit swallowed food. After a bite of tainted food, a rat becomes bait-shy. Word spreads quickly through the colonies. If one rat gets sick after eating poisoned bait, the entire colony avoids that food in the future.

Once a rat invaded the Alameda county sheriff's office and nibbled at the stash of confiscated marijuana. None of the detectives knew how the rat penetrated the vice squad's concrete-walled, vault-like evidence room, but all noticed it had a voracious appetite. In one day the rat munched through three baggies of *sensimilla*, enough, one detective said, "to keep a nice-sized party going for a couple of days."

At that alarming rate, detectives grew nervous that their evidence would evaporate before the felon who harvested the pot could be brought to trial.

To catch the rat intruder detectives set a trap baited with muenster cheese laced with rat poison. But the rat, content with his marijuana diet, didn't touch the bait. The detectives spent the better part of a week on and off duty discussing alternate methods to curb the rat's appetite. A cat could patrol the vault after hours. Was there a poisonous gas they could use? A chemical repellent?

For two nights, judging by the rat droppings deposited near the trap, the rat came back looking for marijuana.

"If you're stoned," one detective said to another, "what

would you want to eat? Cheese doesn't cut it."

"Lemon meringue pie!"

"Get real. You can't fit a piece of pie in a trap."

"Angel food cake!"

"Too spongy."

"How about peanut butter?"

"Peanut butter...got it!"

On the third night the nutty aroma of peanuts blended into a creamy paste was tempting. The rat circled the area looking for marijuana but finding none he nibbled at the tainted nut butter. That night in the sealed vault of the sheriff's office the rat fell into his last chemically induced stupor from which he never awoke.

When the trial date arrived the contraband gardener—who rigged up his basement with 600 watt bulbs, a network of hoses and a fire-extinguisher-sized tank of carbon dioxide to spray over the foliage to stimulate quick marijuana growth—was convicted.

After the judge ordered the felon sent to prison, a deputy sheriff transported what was left of the evidence, the dwindling marijuana stash, to a hospital incinerator. He set fire to the dried weed and carefully stoked the flames of the basement incinerator, relieved to complete the case.

He soon learned one of the drawbacks of burning a large amount of marijuana. Above the hospital smokestack a flock of barn sparrows flew headlong into an immense wafting marijuana cloud. The birds became so intoxicated they collided with small planes landing and taking off at the county airport five miles out of town.

AN ELEPHANT'S PET RAT

Rats play prominent roles in eastern myths and legends. When Lord Buddha gave one of his sermons the rat was the first to arrive. Impressed, the Buddha designated the first year in a cycle of twelve years to be known as the *Year of the Rat.*

Hindus worship the elephant-headed deity Ganesh who overcomes obstacles and brings good luck. Ganesh's favorite companion, the one who follows him everywhere, is his pet rat.

Ganesh is not a whole elephant. Only his head is an elephant's. The rest of his body is rotund and pudgy; attributes, which look adorable on a baby, but odd, attached to an elephant's head.

Ganesh had a difficult childhood. His mother, the goddess Paravati, loved him dearly. His father Shiva, however, grew jealous when he saw how much attention Pavarati showered on Ganesh. One day in a fit of wild dancing Shiva's matted dreadlocks arching out from his head caught fire. Every time he twirled, sparks flew off into the forest igniting wildfires. Creatures ran for cover as the god Shiva stormed home to the palace he shared on Mt. Kailash with his family.

"Who is that handsome young man in my bedroom?" he fumed.

In a blind rage, before his tearful wife could stop him, Shiva cut off his son's head.

"You beheaded our son!" Paravati screamed."You crazy blind fool! Oh, my son. My poor baby. Get out!"

When Shiva realized his mistake, he grew remorseful and wanted to appease his wife. He also feared that one day his son might seek his own revenge. With or without heads, gods and goddesses in the Hindu pantheon are immortal. Shiva promised to reattach the head, but where did he toss it? He searched high and low throughout the universe. The boy's handsome head was nowhere to be found.

He spotted an elephant grazing on the terrain just below his cave abode on Mt. Kailash. Desperate to locate a head he whipped out his hunting knife and whacked off the elephant's head with one swift blow. Then he reattached the head atop his son's body. Some say he could have looked harder. What kind of substitution is an elephant's head for a handsome young prince?

Ganesh grew up happy but distrustful. Who could blame him? If his own father beheaded him, who could he trust? His favorite pet rat, both companion and partner, accompanied him everywhere. The rat's cunning helped Ganesh get out of difficult scrapes.

Once when the floodwaters of the Ganges rose rapidly stranding Ganesh on an island midstream, the rat swam through the snarling rapids to summon help. Another time Ganesh dropped a bracelet down a rabbit-hole and the rat jumped down to retrieved it. They became as inseparable as mother and child.

Other deities could ride on their animal mounts like Durga on her lion and Shiva with the bull Nandi but if Ganesh tried to ride on his small rat, he'd flatten him like road kill. Nevertheless they became steadfast partners.

Their teamwork became legendary. When Ganesh crashed through the forest he ripped off the highest, most tenderest tree branches to eat while the rat burrowed underground, tunneling passages into granaries and larders. With their combined strength and wit they conquered all obstacles, high and low, near and far.

RAT PANTHEON

At some Ganesh mandirs or temples, the rat that accompanies the elephant-headed Hindu deity is sometimes enlarged a hundredfold so Ganesh can sit astride the rat's ample back. Mostly the rat peers out between Ganesh's pudgy feet ready to disappear into a tunnel underground or hop up on his master's knee.

Sharing an honored spot in the Hindu pantheon is a distant cousin-in-appearance to the rat, the mongoose, a favored pet of another deity, Jambhala, the God of Wealth.

The similarity between a rat and a mongoose is only visual, however, since a mongoose's favorite meal is a nice plump rat. On altars all over India the pampered mongoose cuddles in Lord Jambhala's spacious, silk-draped lap. The royal mongoose appears smug, fully satiated, no doubt, after a recent meal of a fat, juicy rat.

When a mongoose feasts on a rat, he greedily chews up the entire body: ears, bones, fur, tail, claws and teeth, scrunching, burping, swallowing every last morsel.

What accounts for the origin of the myth about the precious jewels the mongoose burps up into the Lord of Wealth's spacious lap? Is it after relishing a rat meal that the royal mongoose belches shiny gems from the depths of his rotund furry, belly? Does the mongoose regurgitate half-digested rat cud that miraculously transforms into coveted gems? Does a mongoose possess a magical alchemic stomach that turns rat carcasses into beautiful gemstones on a deity's altar?

MAHARAJA'S LAMENT

Even with his favorite rat, Ganesh is cautious. If a father can cut off his son's head, a pet might turn on his master. Just because a rat is small, Ganesh thinks, as he remembered a childhood story, doesn't mean a rat can't harm or destroy.

At one time the Maharaja of Rajpur kept his favorite elephant, Rudra, tethered to a banyan tree during long visits at his summer palace by the shore. One morning the Maharaja's elephant keeper came to him, "Sir, we must move the elephant's tether. At night a vicious rat attacks him."

"Don't be absurd. A rat attack an elephant?"

"He bites the elephant's feet."

"No rat bite can bother a mighty elephant. That's ridiculous. Stop wasting my time with your idle pratter. Get back to work."

The next morning the elephant keeper returned, this time he was more agitated. "Your honor, again the rat came. He is so small and fast, he takes a bite and runs off. If the elephant was quicker he could step on him but you know how slow elephants are. They can't see well at night, either."

"Don't waste my time with preposterous rat tales. To an elephant, a rat bite is no worse than a mosquito bite for us."

A week went by and the Maharaja asked the elephant keeper to report back to him."Tell me. How is the elephant this week? Are the mango leaves to his liking?"

"Sir, he hasn't eaten in a day. As I told you, the rat attacks him every night. After two nights he bit a hole through the tough skin the size of a nutmeg seed. The small hole became infected. Sir, we need a doctor, fast."

"A doctor? Let me see this infection."

The keeper led the Maharaja to the elephant's yard where they found the mighty elephant prostrate on the ground. The infection spread rapidly and within hours he died from the untreated wound.

If the Maharaja didn't see for himself the sorry state of his favorite elephant, he never would have believed that a small rat could cause the downfall of the king of the forest.

What Lemmings Know

Distant rodent cousins of the rat, the lemmings, cluster for the winters in a colony dug beneath pine groves in the mountains of Norway. Not every spring or every other spring but at a time they deem crucial, lemmings may emerge outside the colony en masse in broad daylight to assemble in a long line.

Hundreds join to march together. As the crow flies, the lemmings tramp, like soldiers to a battlefield. Neither house nor creek, road nor lake impedes their progress.

Unarmed they do not fight each other or enemies along the way. Is the sea a destination? Or does the sea rise, siren-like, an immense obstacle or distraction on the path?

Their walk is not a protest or political statement.

Does fuzzy vision guide them? Nocturnal nibbling on potent fungi or fermented berries may induce dreams of underwater worlds, offshore havens.

Is the urge to travel the result of impaired judgment? A chemical imbalance or dietary deficiency?

Unexplained longings may drive, lure some from the safety of a communal burrrow. To experience life in a new element or territory may prompt a mass exodus. Wanderlust has no schedule or fixed destination. Nor does primordial atavistic yearnings.

Some say the trek is planned. That lemmings are the epitome of conscientious social creatures whose actions benefit the colony. When overpopulation crowds their mountain habitat, seasonal migration may relieve the problem. A mass departure alleviates overcrowded conditions in the underground warren.

Others contend the critters suffer an hormonal imbalance that stimulates a craving for death. Some may choose suicide in the company of friends and relatives like whales who beach themselves en masse on a shore.

It's possible, too, that common stupidity misguides them. The gullible may follow a false prophet who preaches a pilgrim's path to the plentiful harvests of rat Xanadu and bountiful fields of a rodent Shambhala.

Lemmings are excellent swimmers—they can tread water—but their skills pale in the frigid waters of a Nordic sea. After three days without ground to stand on or food, scores drown within a mile of land. Bodies wash ashore.

Some may swim to an uncharted island. A few might hitch rides on dolphins' backs. Still others like Jonah may settle down, keep house inside a whale's belly.

THE IDOLATRY OF RAT FLESH

To many a rat carcass is a filthy, disease-ridden disgusting mass. The humble burying beetle, on the other hand, whose diet consists of rotting carrion, holds a rat corpse in high esteem.

It is a good day of scavenging when a burying beetle locates a rat specimen not already swollen and puffy in the ripe stages of putrefaction. Maybe the lucky beetle reaps the rewards of a morally upright life; or reaps the benevolence of the Great Provider in the Ground. In a beetle's carrion diet, a black or brown rat is prime cuisine.

Like the rat that sneaks around in the shadows to pilfer and prey upon another's bounty, a burying beetle sneaks about the fields and lots, searching for dead meat that is not already claimed by ferret or wolf. No beetle will wage battle to obtain the prized flesh. It's only natural that rats, tillers of the soil, diggers of tunnels whose teeth penetrate wood, metal, stumps, and sewer pipes, come to be idolized in the realm they know best, the underground recesses of the earth.

When a burying beetle finds a dead rat, transportation is out of the question since a rat is an immense creature, hundreds of times larger in size and weight of a single beetle. With luck a rat dies on an arable portion of soil. Gravediggers by training, sextons by calling, the beetles move clumps of soil, push by push, out from under the rat. The rat is interred by eliminating the dirt directly beneath the body, in the exact spot where the rat expired. No separate burial hole is necessary.

In a matter of hours a rat is lowered into a depression in the ground, whereupon the beetle deposits eggs. After hurriedly pushing the dirt on top of the carcass, the burial is complete. The rumpled dirt of a small hillock is all that remains on the surface of the earth.

Within two weeks a carcass transforms into a hairless black slimy mass exuding colorful green, yellow and brown pus. Working quickly to beat the onset of inevitable decay, the beetle larvae feast and grow. Ripe with nourishment, incandescent with putrefaction, the white burrowing grubs emerge from the stinking rotting mess.

Within ten days the larvae become nymphs, and soon after adult beetles. The scent and flavor of mouthfuls of rotten rat meat indelibly marks a young beetle's memory. Those savory morsels which first nourished their young bodies now define the essence of all future diets: the ooze of rotting rat flesh, the murk of decomposing gut, the gentle swell of putrescence.

Young burying beetles practice an idolatry of rat flesh. When they burrow out of their carcass nest, step above ground and begin their life of scavenging, their appetites harbor a secret craving for the pablum of childhood, the idyllic womb of nourishment, the rotting rat corpse. In this way the idolatry of rat flesh, the succulent ooze of rotting rat gut, the smoldering rot and fetid flesh, is established in the underground burial chambers of the humble burying beetle.

Eco Rats

Despite worldwide protests a country recently tested an atomic bomb on a remote Pacific atoll. The blast decimated all life on the island. Deadly radioactive fallout covered the ground. It would be years before any visible signs of life could return.

The bomb blast terrified the island rats. Half of their tunnels collapsed. An intense heat filtered down from above and scorched the ground of their shallowest tunnels. Only those who tunneled hundreds of feet down, boring tunnels through the very heart-bone of the coral-encrusted atoll survived.

For years wise elder rats warned of a famine, a time of cataclysmic hurricanes destroying the island. Rats began to stock their underground chambers with dried coconut meat, dried fish and bananas. They augmented supplies by burrowing under trees to eat roots and insect grubs. They drank from underground pools. They stored enough food to last two or three rat generations.

Eventually the island rats' supply of buried foodstuffs dwindled. Curiosity overwhelmed rats born after the blast. In small numbers rat scouts began to poke their noses above ground, sniff the air, scan the beaches for washed up fish.

As they dig new tunnels, they turn the soil over and over, mixing and burying the toxic fallout and releasing nutrient-rich, unspoiled earth from deep underground.

In this way rats play a role in recovering land after a nuclear catastrophe. In the next millennium when the meek are destined to inherit, rats will become guides, act as gurus and be treated like saints.

FOUR
HOUSE OF GLASS

HOUSE OF FLEAS

It's easy to pluck fleas off my skin. I can feel the smallest flea land. Their black bodies, some so tiny, stand out in contrast to my pale flesh. When I'm tired I start grabbing at the few black moles on my legs thinking they're fleas. I should have memorized where the moles are by now.

After my housemate Sally got a new job, she and her cat Henrietta moved out. The first morning after their departure the house felt lighter. But when I came downstairs to start the coffee pot in the kitchen something tickled my ankles. Kettle in hand, I leaned over and counted seven tiny black dots climbing my legs.

That damn cat! Swatting only sent the fleas hopping. In no time they were back, crawling up the slopes of my ankles. Without Henrietta around to nurture the baby fleas, they went wild attacking me. One floated in my morning coffee cup. I almost swallowed it. If only Henrietta took the pests with her.

The fleas didn't actually bite me. I ate too much garlic for their taste. It's Trevor they bothered. They loved his blood. Every time he came over tiny red bites showed up on his legs. We talked about living together but he won't move into a house with fleas.

Trevor, a pacifist, doesn't believe in killing. I admire his conviction. I don't believe in killing insects either but I distinguish between good insects and bad insects. Also, I'm a master at compromise. I put up with adversity longer than he can, hoping to find a solution. Patience is a skill I acquired. He says I just put blinders up to avoid confrontation.

"What's wrong with avoiding confrontation?" I counter. "I'm a pacifist at heart, too."

At first I developed a squishing technique. If a flea hopped on me as I sat down to eat, I caught it between my thumb and forefinger. Then I pulled back on my thumb a little and with my forefinger nailed the flea tight against my skin. Then I pressed and pressed, tighter and tighter, until the nail added the final touch. Only when a flea was split in half, was it a goner. Otherwise I squeezed and squeezed but their hard-shelled bodies resisted the pressure.

This method worked for a flea or two, but was totally unsatisfactory if there were dozens. If my leg had ten fleas, say, I could only nab one at a time. The others escaped. The method wasn't foolproof either. My fingernail didn't always pin down a flea. Some fleas were super fast and hopped away before the nail clamped down. Sometimes my first grip was off and I missed. Other times I wasn't sure if I had a flea between thumb and forefinger until I peeked and unintentionally set it free.

Sally regularly gave Henrietta an herbal flea bath in the kitchen sink, cooing, "There, there Etta. I don't like this any better than you do."

After the herbal bath she strung an herbal flea collar around Henrietta's neck and lit incense. She bought fleabane to plant near the house to discourage the fleas from entering, but the fleabane died before Sally got around to planting it. Then Sally had one of her heart-to-heart talks with her pet.

"Etta this powder will get rid of the fleas. Hold still. I'll be gentle. It won't hurt. Trust me."

"Cats listen," Sally claimed. "It's good to talk to them."

Before they moved, Sally told Henrietta all about the new home; that she need not worry, she would be fed, and loved, and happy there."She adjusted perfectly," Sally told me on the phone, "without incident." Sally forgot to whisper into Henrietta's ears before they moved: "Bring the fleas with you. It will be all right. They need you, Henrietta. There's plenty of room for all of us in our new home."

A week after they left there were so many fleas at my ankles, picking them off to crush one by one was futile. Trevor hated bombs and poisonous sprays. I agreed with his reasoning. If we bombed the house with insecticide our air would be contaminated with noxious chemicals. Trevor worried about the effect on other unsuspecting and helpful insects like spiders.

I wondered what the life span of a flea was, or how long could flea eggs keep hatching baby fleas. Then in desperation I opened the window and just dropped them outdoors as fast as I caught them. It was easy, painless. I caught fifteen in no time and tossed them outside.

"When you pick me up come right in," I told Trevor. "The door's unlocked."

I wanted to say, "Hurry before the fleas hop a ride back in on your pant leg." There's a drawback to dropping fleas out the window. They're outside but for how long?

"I'll honk," he said. "I'm not coming inside." We went to a movie and he dropped me off out front after.

"Come inside for coffee?"

He shook his head.

"What do you want me to do?"

"Get rid of the fleas."

"But how? You don't want me to spray."

"There's a powder you shake on rugs. Maybe that will work."

The next morning as I lay in bed thinking of methods to get rid of other household pests like ants or mice an idea came to me. I remembered some advice on ticks a neighbor, Reverend Hutch, once gave me.

"Get a glass bottle, a small jar," he said. "Fill it an inch or two with rubbing alcohol. When you pull a tick off drop it into the alcohol. Saves squashing them." He showed off his small medicine bottle of pickled ticks he pulled off the thick fur of his Siamese. He swished around the liquid so the dark bodies twirled like ballerinas in the clear alcohol. Christians, I gathered, had no qualms about exterminating insects. We agreed squashing bugs was a nasty business. Tick bodies were hard and armored like flea bodies but a hundred times larger.

I didn't have any rubbing alcohol in the house. Could I substitute something else? What about bleach?

In the cupboard beneath the sink I pulled out a half-gallon white plastic bleach bottle and poured a little in a cup. At breakfast I picked any fleas off my ankles and dropped them, one at a time, into a ceramic coffee mug filled to a depth of one inch with bleach. Catching was easy, as long as I didn't have to squish. The fleas kicked around awhile then settled down. A few tried to climb the sides but after I swished the bleach around in the mug, they sank to the bottom of the cup. I counted the catch that morning: fourteen fleas. A record I'd rather forget. When I came back that afternoon, the dozens I left swimming in the cup of bleach were nowhere to be seen. They completely vanished.

"Those bastards!" I complained on the phone to Trevor.

"Now what?"

"They outsmarted me by playing dead."

"What?"

"When I left the kitchen, they climbed out of the mug, shook off the bleach and hopped away."

"They're dead. Look again. Fleas can't survive a dunk in bleach."

"But they'd leave a trace." The bleach left in the cup was as pure and clear as when I first poured it in.

"Trace? What kind of trace are you looking for, insects dissolving in an acid bath?"

"Their shells bleached white. That's it. They're invisible in the white coffee mug."

"You're telling me you have invisible fleas?"

"Either that or they left voluntarily."

"Call me when they gone," he said and hung up.

"They're gone," I called the next day. "I swear."

I didn't count; numbers were depressing. But every flea that landed within reach ended up in the bleach. I never figured out what became of them after the immersion. Trevor inspected the mug and he couldn't find any trace either. There were no more tickles at my ankles. Without the tiny inhabitants the house seemed happier, friendlier.

I no longer pause on the porch dreading to open the front door.

A Hex on Roaches

I'm cooped up in my loft for the third day with nothing but bone soup to nurse a wounded stomach but I reached an understanding that I wouldn't otherwise have if I had gone out into the market and streets of this blurry, snowed in city. The understanding is this: there are lessons to be learned when contemplating the afterlife of vermin, especially those perennially adaptable cockroaches that never seem to completely die out no matter how often I set baited roach traps out.

Roaches thrived during the days of the dinosaurs; they left their skeletons firmly embedded and fossilized in stone. Later they spread throughout Europe during the Greek and Roman empires and flourished in the Middle Ages. Today their progeny are firmly ensconced in the inner walls and underground passages of many homes and apartments, especially those in large cities and some medium sized cities like mine.

Cockroaches first made a literary appearance in the ancient seventy-two foot long Egyptian papyrus scroll, *The Book of the Dead*, where the great god Knun, the primeval creator of the earth, uttered a personal spell to ward off the creatures. His spell is simple and direct:

"Be far from me, O vile cockroach,
For I am the God Knun..."

Why the creator of the earth and presumably the creatures on it, had to cast a spell to ward off one of his own creations? Beats me.

Roaches have a perseverance that's enviable. Once I visited a friend who lived down south. During lunch a large cockroach appeared under the table. He prowled around on the floor as we ate, waiting for a wayward grain of rice or other morsel to drop. Then he picked up the scrap and diligently attempted to transport it to some private place, a home or nest, perhaps, away from the commotion of the kitchen.

The path the cockroach took led directly up the kitchen wall. Normally he easily scaled this perpendicular surface. The addition of a single grain of rice, however, threw his balance off. He only managed to climb two feet up the wall, before dropping the grain. Undaunted, he scurried back down and tried again but only to meet with the same fate. Again and again. After eight tries, he quit. However amused I was to chart the peregrinations of this tropical Sisyphean creature, I was secretly grateful the enormous three-inch variety didn't hang out in my kitchen.

In all the apartments I've lived in, the roaches were fond of the hum and whir of little motors. They love warm, squeaky electric vibrations, the breath and purr of little spinning wheels and cogs. Roaches always swarm and vie for space within the complexity and security of small domestic motors that never turn off like the refrigerator or the electric wall clock. It's hard to imagine pre-industrial roaches without machinery to inhabit.

Yesterday I began to type my new manuscript. I put in a new sheet of paper and was midway into the second sentence about a dung beetle, another Egyptian insect, this one consumed with the promethean task of rolling a great ball of dung up hill and down, when the typewriter acted up.

The typewriter was an electric model that I rented by the

month since I didn't have money to invest in a word processor nor the patience to frequent the public library to use theirs. The rental typed the letters that corresponded to the keys my fingers punched, but it added a touch of it's own. A splash of color, I should say, like the beginning of a Jackson Pollock drip painting.

Right at the beginning of the third sentence of the second paragraph a swirl of orange smeared the words the ribbon typed. A color rather like a rusty sunset or a rotting orange peel, surrounded a yellowish red.

At the time I was angry. Machines, by nature, by definition, by mechanical law, should only perform in a prescribed way. To add color to a poem or words to a painting or miles to a speedometer, without the express designation of the poet, artist or driver, was acting out of line. What business did a typewriter have in throwing color into my story? Even if only a dash of color.

If it wasn't ten o'clock in the morning I might have mistaken this apparition for some sort of hallucination like the kind I get after a late dinner when there is food in the pantry and wine in the carafe. When I stare into a fire images dance in the flames. A tree's legacy is written in the flames of its demise. A knothole, for example, remains darker in the midst of the smoldering fire. Outer bark flares rapidly, its ashen silhouette disperses and doen't linger leisurely like the solid coals of the heartwood.

But this was too early in the day for such illusions. Clearly my eyes weren't playing tricks. The color was real and growing in dimension. By the third line the moisture on the paper caused the letters to bleed together.

Of all the times possible, why was the machine acting

up now? Was the motor leaking oil? If the typewriter was broken, for whatever reason, luckily I wouldn't be responsible for it's repair. Another reason to rent a machine; rental contracts covered repairs.

By now the sheet of paper with the half-written paragraph was useless since moisture spoiled the surface. The color certainly would not rub or scrape off. I'd have to begin again. For one brief moment I enjoyed the display: the yellow was edged with a red border, and the splotch seeped from a central point outward, like waves in a pool or lake, rippling towards the shore.

When I pulled the paper from the machine and turned it over I discovered the source of the problem. A flattened roach dangled from the backside. The roach was trapped between roller and the paper. Unwittingly each letter I typed further squashed the insect. If the cockroach had cried out, I would have been warned and stopped typing. But that was not the case. The more I typed, the more the letters pressed the vital fluids out, creating the colors on my clean white typing sheet.

At least the typewriter wasn't on the verge of malfunction. The machine couldn't be held accountable. The roach no doubt was so attracted to the humming of the typewriter motor that it nested in the inner recesses of the machine, waiting for those precious moments when the motor kicked in, stirred to life.

I was about to toss the paper in the trash when I remembered the god Knun's incantation:

"Be Far From Me, O vile cockroach."

In a flash I penciled his words on the paper and tacked it to the wall. The roaches will find it. They often scurry up and down these walls. At the least a curious roach will sniff the ink of the typed letters and smell the odor of the lifeless, squashed roach that wandered inadvertently inside the typewriter where he met his demise. By the powers of scent alone a sensitive insect will figure that the two, that is, typewriter inks and cockroaches, don't mix. A smart insect will make a further assumption: Death comes to trespassers.

GARDEN MENAGERIE

After my pet turtle died, his squat empty glass bowl begged for a new tenant. Every day on the way to catch the school bus I passed the bowl in the sideyard where I abandoned it after Charlie died. Slimy moss tinged the sides of his bowl green. Leaves from the loquat tree fell in, browned, then blacked into a limp pile of rot. Over the winter I gauged rainfall by the level of water collected in the wide mouthed bowl.

I had failures before. Gold fish floated belly up in their bowl. A starfish from Moss Beach stunk up the patio after it died. Now I know not to catch another starfish or sea anenome.

For a day I entertained myself with a Japanese paper garden I bought in a toy shop in Chinatown by the bay. The instructions were printed on the thinest sheet of cheap newsprint paper about two inches long. I ignored the Japanese lettering I couldn't read, but the pictures were clear: slip off the thin paper ring holding two miniature clam shells and contents together; hold empty glass under pouring faucet; drop clam shell package in the glass; wait five minutes. A little wind up alarm clock with two bells on top told me that.

One, two...the shell opened alittle. Water seeped inside and soaked tightly rolled paper coils. Three, four...coils unfurled in the water and floated upwards like bubbles. Soon red and yellow flower petals, pointy green leaves and grass or weeds hovered in the water. It was magical. If I shook the glass to make tiny waves the paper flowers quivered in the water like seaweed.

The abandoned scummy bowl outside all winter depressed me. But come spring I scrubbed the bowl crystal clear again and biked to Lake Lagunitas with an empty jar in my bike basket. No polywogs. I trapped two tiny frogs which would be happy in a new private home of their own. Baby ferns, a few rocks, an inch of water with a large rock island to sun themselves on. What could be more comfortable? A piece of screen over the top to prevent escape.

I sacrificed two sow bugs. I say sacrificed since they're my favorite armor-shelled insects that roll up into perfect BB sized balls, each segmented like peeled oranges into eight or twelve wedges. I loved to roll a few back and forth slinky-like between cupped palms. Sow bugs that crawled around under logs in the yard never got dizzy.

On the other hand, if I could catch a few flying bugs the frogs could whip out their long tongues and snag their own dinner. Flies might be good, too, but I don't like swatting flies and carrying any carcasses out to the bowl. I tried that once. Killing isn't my thing.

In the bug world flies are outcastes. If they didn't relish shit, blood-oozed meat, the vilest carrion, yellow mucus, pus or fetid garbage, they might be persuaded to become pets and chirp like crickets in a bamboo cage in a classroom solarium. Or flies could be trained like circus fleas to hop, kick balls, play games to amuse people. If they hid their lusting after the most noxious spoilage they might pass as innocuous insects.

I switched the wire screen over the frogs' bowl for one with wider square openings to allow flies to crawl through. To attract enough flies for a couple of frog meals—something gross—raw hamburger meat!

The menagerie kept me busy for about a week. Long enough for the meat to rot and the frogs escape. Don't ask me why the flies didn't go for the meat or how the frogs escaped. They just did. At least Charlie's old turtle bowl didn't turn into a frog morgue or holding tank for specimens in a science dissecting lab and I didn't have to perform frog burials under the loquat tree.

MIGRATION OF WORMS

The year the rains arrived on the back of a hideous monsoon madman water pelted down so forcefully babies screamed. Dogs howled as wild, unleashed branches thundered against the houses of the town.

After a night's deluge that was hard to measure except in terms of persistence, the worms silently poked their heads above their underground hideouts. When drumming rain and floodwaters filled their tunnels they emerged swimming in their eel incarnations.

As the worms left the confinement of their earthen digs, assortments of skinny creatures assembled on the periphery of the road near the sea. They formed regiments, divided into phalanxes, began an impossible traverse on the asphalt plane.

There was a pattern, a consistency to their movements. They headed south on the sloping road; they traveled from left to right. No one knew when they began or why, or how many cleared the hazardous concourse under cover of dark but at daybreak those left on the rigid, coated surface stopped dead, caught midway in a silent, nocturnal pilgrimage.

In the morning slimy glints trailed the sun, elongated bodies stilled in crazy poses. Did they play dead? Maybe they thought they were invisible if they stopped moving. Did the blinding light of day paralyze them, like deer caught off guard in the high beams of headlights on dark forest roads?

From the dungeons in their inland village, the rats

sniffed the sea air. When the wind exuded a saline scent and the moist breath of the sea fanned the rats' whiskers, they abandoned their nests to journey a day and a night. Rats knew by the sea scent, the rain breeze, when the worms began their journey. On the way, many stopped in fields to feed on corn and millet. Some never finished the trek, but others trudged on fueled by fond memories of licking juicy creatures, tender as steamed snails, off the pavement.

If a worm lived through the day and into the night, it might continue its mysterious migration towards some primordial spring ritual like an underground feast or gathering. Each year the rats scurried to intercept the worms' spring ritual with a primordial ritual feast of their own.

HOUSE OF GLASS

The house of glass had double walls like an ant farm, only the walls were much taller and full of water instead of dirt. Double glass panes, like storm windows, rose from the floor to cap off the second story, a massive transparent dome. Instead of pockets of air, warm tropical water filled the six-inch gap between panes. Turquoise and chartreuse fish with golden fins swam these narrow corridors.

Along the bottom of the glass walls, masses of tiny bubbles constantly drifted skyward. You could see out but no one could see through the bubble curtain. It was like living in an aquarium except bubbles masked the view in.

When it rained, drops hammered the glass dome overhead, then waterfalled, slid down the sides. On really hot days the dome sweated beads of condensation.

Even the floor was transparent. A slab of thick foundation glass rested directly on the ground. If you shined a bright spotlight when you peered down, worms, grubs, and serpents turned in their sleep.

In the moonlight the whole house glowed with iridescence.

FIVE
CAGED ANIMALS

CLOUDS

Above her bungalow in the Himalayas rain clouds drift high above the plains every afternoon as they nudge north. Clouds puff in silently, sneak all the way up to Crank's Ridge, a climb of three thousand feet. Slowly white vapors fill the cavernous valley and blanket the forested ridges until the only thing visible is the everpresent thick, billowy angel breath.

When the American opens her front door the sky tiptoes in on cotton slippers. The monsoons arrive but never on a set schedule. Deluge after deluge brushes the dust from the leaves, windows.

In the bazaar, dogs, birds and people seek shelter, cower under overhangs and eaves. Water in sheets and showers plunks out the rhythms of descent on the tin roof over her head.

Monsoon

One year intense monsoon inundations swamp the dry grassy high altitude meadow. Violent and thunderous storms pound at the door. Water cascades down dried up waterfall beds, invigorating jungles of dormant skeletal weeds. Downpours slam the earth twice a day; some last the entire day.

The American diverts the runoff from the corrugated roof into a large barrel to use for cooking, drinking and bathing. Otherwise a walk to the nearest spring is over a mile, too far to lug water in a pail.

The mud floor and walls of the bungalow soften like butter.

Leather shoes and belts sprout tinges of green mold. Ink seeps unpredictably into the moist notebook paper in her journal, blurring the words like blotting paper.

To dry clothes she suspends garments over a wire hoop that fits over a charcoal brazier in the room.

A Flood in the Bungalow

One night the drainage ditch on the road above the bungalow breaks. Muddy water careens downhill carving a stream to the kitchen door where it slips, seeping inside. Water creeps over the mud floor then cascades into the studio where the American sleeps on the floor. She wakes to the sound of a small waterfall four feet from her head.

She gropes in the dark to light the kerosene lantern then quickly gathers the bedding to keep it from soaking up water like a dry sponge.

Armed with a shovel she scrambles barefoot up the mountain of mud to the road. Wiping rain from her brow with the crook of her arm, she digs a new channel away from the entrenched path through her kitchen. Rain pellets sting, pound against the shovel.

For days she steps on blocks of wood placed strategically on the mud floor. To get from the living room to the kitchen requires a balancing act or else a foot sinks into the brown squishy mess.

Moisture seeps into her pores, permeates her skin, her clothes. The bottom half of her straw mattress reeks of mold at night every time she turns over in bed. A weekly hot mustard oil massage from the masseuse in the bazaar temporarily alleviates her aching bones, but her joints are stiff for months.

THE ANGREZI

In the bazaar the merchants call the American who eats and drinks like a local, the *Angrezi* or Anglo in the local dialect. She is the *Angrezi* who lives, cooks and sleeps as a native, the foreigner adrift in their world.

The *Angrezi* buys an ancient sedative in the apothecary shop. She carries the black glob wrapped in plastic in a tiny silver matchbox size pillbox in a leather pouch attached to her belt. Dragons entwine on the silver lid; their eyes embedded corals from Kathmandu. Inside wrapped in a plastic sheath the gooey black opium gum.

With her thumbnail she breaks off a small bit. Her body shudders with heat, nausea and the acrid, bitter aftertaste. The monsoon arthritis that permeates her bones eases into a slow retreat.

THE SHRINE

Inside the temple the *Angrezi* nudges into the throng slowly inching their way into the presence of *Durga*, the wrathful resident Goddess. Crowds knock, rub shoulders, shove against each other. Reverberations of thick brass donging temple bells roust pigeons from the eaves. In between the priest's recitations devotees shout: "Hurry up! Get out of the way!"

The *Angrezi* stops in front of the image of a crazy long black-haired Mother Goddess from whose angry mouth a blood dripping tongue wags ghoulishly. A string of severed demon heads—a tantric necklace—adorns her chest. Her arms grip, flash deadly weapons.

"Who is this bloody-tongued Goddess?" the *Angrezi* wonders.

The intoxicating allure of vertigo swirls in an inebriating stupor.

THIEVES

Beware of pickpockets!

—sign in English and Hindi on the temple wall

A re thieves so bold they steal from a house of worship? What is the punishment for those who rob the devoted, for those who lust for the riches of others in a sacred place?

The *Angrezi* presses her elbow against her shoulder bag so tightly she can't inhale without feeling her wallet safely poke her rib cage. She is amazed, not by the threat of having her wallet stolen, but by the peopled frenzy in the *Durga* temple, spiritual fervor gone awry.

In this country, she thinks, holy days are frequent and religious crowds a constant presence in the streets and temples. In mass bathing rites at the rivers and in holy parades on festival days Hindus jostle and pray at the same time. A crazed spirituality permeates every crowd.

Madness

At the *Durga* temple the mundane and the spiritual not only coexist, they nurture each other. In the confusion and the chaos lie seeds of the divine. Likewise the divine image of the ferocious deity manifests chaos.

The thick aroma of burning sandalwood incense intoxicates. Confusion overwhelms the *Angrezi* as simultaneous and incongruous activity erupts from every direction, every corner.

Pickpockets thrive when the crowds shove and push. She yearns to bring order to the confusion. If only the devotees could pass through turnstiles, she thinks, the scene might be orderly.

In the iconography of Christianity, Jesus, Mary and all of the saints maintain and display benign countenances. There is not an angry face among them, nor does anyone sport more than the usual number of limbs. There is no pantheon in Christianity, either. There is one male God, his son and the woman who birthed him.

The appearance of the blood-drooling, snarling, many-armed, witchy Goddess bewilders.

Namaste

When worshipers come before a Goddess in her temple, they naturally bow their heads in respect and press palms together in obeisance. Likewise strangers who meet for the first time fold their palms together and exchange the greeting, *namaste*. Everyone *namastes*.

Temple-goers greet the resident Gods and Goddesses with *namaste*. Friends salute friends with *namaste*. Even merchants in the bazaar *namaste* to foreign customers who enter their shops.

Greeting a deity as you would an old friend adds an informal, personal touch. After the *Angrezi namastes* in the temple, the priest places a red mark on her forehead and offers her a small glob of milk sweet, the *prasad* offering she blindly swallows like a prescribed drug.

Worshipers exit the temple backwards to always face the shrine with folded palms. It is bad luck to turn your back to the altar.

At the entrance with heads still lowered the devotees slip their feet back into the shoes left outside the temple door. They nudge their way out between crowds pressing forward for their turn to stand before the deity's presence.

Buffalo

The village was lush once. Ancient scriptures illuminate exotically painted birds and forests thick with trees and foliage. Every afternoon a herd of water buffalos stampede to the river, plow into the brown shimmering liquid.

When the *Angrezi* stares into the liquidy eyes of a water buffalo tethered far away from the river, she sees the distant memory of a river, of life before drought, before deforestation. The slow droop of a buffalo's eyelid, lashes as long as paint brushes, reminds her of sleeping angels. The buffalo blink makes her sad.

She drinks buffalo milk thick as custard and pure as the ghostly snow on distant peaks. When the *Angrezi* scoops cream thick like cream cheese from the top of her milk pail, she thinks of the rich, sweet ambrosic *amrita* the Gods churn.

MAHARAJA

When the *Angrezi* sunbathes on the sandstone steps of the Ganges in Hardwar, her long damp hair clumps into dozens of wavy strands. Oil of coconut saturates her skin. Temple bells clang in the distance. Surely this sunny spot on the *ghat* of a holy river drifting south is better than a forest retreat, she thinks.

A passing shadow eclipses the light falling across her body. She looks up. A man wearing shades and a gold necklace stands before her.

"Shri Govinda Das, Maharaja of Hardiwar," he announces bowing slightly with palms together in the customary greeting. He wears fine white silk *pajamas* and a loose whispy silk *kurta* that deflects the sun's sheen.

"If you return for the *mela*," he says after they chat awhile, "I invite you to stay in my palace." He motions to a tall fort-like structure behind him on the river bank. The Maharaja's property overlooks the most sacred spot in the city.

"During the *mela* pilgrims sing, pray and dip in the water at his very spot," he says nodding to the stone steps leading down to the river. "They squeeze tightly together, pour streams of water over their bodies from brass *lota* water pots.

"Hotels and *dharamsalas* were booked solid five years ago. You will not find other lodging. Come as my guest."

CAGED ANIMALS

Six months after her visit to the holy city on the banks of the sacred Ganges, the *Angrezi,* who is also addressed as *memsahib,* returns. Under a nearly full moon, as she steps off the train in Hardwar, a mountain shaped like a squatting buffalo dominates the terrain. Sparse Himalayan scrub reminds her of the scraggly hair on a water buffalo's back.

The lover who lingers in her mind is the one she can't have. In the cool of a shady room her body grips. She dreams of ice and snow falls. Ice shrouds the window; flakes bury the bed, the rug.

A blizzard of her own creation blinds her. Thoughts smother like a blanket. Her body numbs in a false immersion.

In lovemaking she turns inward. Her body generates heat, an antidote to icy environs. But she can't reverse the process. She can't generate cold. Profuse sweat does not cool.

The last time she made love she suspended time, expelled consciousness. As she cried out her expirations gave voice to small animals caged within.

KUMBHA MELA

A steel roar avalanches above the *sadhu* encampment. Every hour a train clambers across the bridge. Pilgrims jam the windows vying for access to toss coins to *Ganga-ji* and the miraculous iron grid. Volunteers round up pilgrims as they descend from the trains. Cholera vaccinations are free and mandatory. There is a zealous wariness and hostility in the crowds.

The village of Hardiwar prepares for the *mela*. Not a half *kumbh,* every twelve years they celebrate a full *Kumbha Mela* in honor of the Sacred Pot dripping with Nectar that the *Devas* churn from the Ocean of Milk. Pilgrims in search of a few drops of this divine elixir arrive from all over India to bathe in the sacred waters of the Ganga.

Overnight tents, bodies and campfires jostle for space, clutter the sandy banks. Thirty million people search for food, firewood, and water. Hungry, cold and thirsty pilgrims wrestle for a spot at the water's edge to worship and bathe.

When an astronaut snaps a picture from space the photograph captures the largest convocation on earth, visible from the moon.

WINDOWS WITHOUT GLASS

Two days before the climax of the massive festival, the Maharaja's cook prepares a lunch of chapati bread, *alu gobi* potato cauliflower curry, mango chutney, spiced yogurt and stuffed deep fried samosas. Guests sit on cushions spread on the marble floor. After *chai* and milk sweets the American returns to watch the crowds from an open air window in her second floor apartment. Iron bars protect against intruders when the wood shutters are open.

The highly polished cement floor glows like the bright red *tikka* dots Hindu women paint on their foreheads. The view overlooks the river at the sacred bathing spot.

A crush of people press forward, garbed in an array of regional costumes representing village, city, tribal, mountain, desert and coastal styles. Women adorned in every variety of cotton, rayon, and sheer, colorful, patterned silk saris brighten the throng like wildflowers on a sand dune. Humble villagers in their freshly laundered handloomed cottons and men in sarongs, pajamas, dhotis, and turbans add to the exotic palette.

Stalled rickshaw drivers struggle to maneuver patrons through the shoulder to shoulder crowd that fills the street at the water's edge. A few sacred cows enter the fray. Rickshaw bells clang angrily. The din and flux of people mesmerizes, absorbs the American's attention.

Hours pass.

INVASIVE

Bathers maneuver, push for a place on the steps of the crowded bathing *ghats* swept clean by perennially bracing, chilly water. The frail grab a chain to keep a precarious balance in the fast moving current. If a pilgrim accidently loses grip, he or she will be swept downriver. A large net stretched under the railway bridge half-a-mile south catches stragglers. Four men with ropes barely manage to free a frightened sacred cow trapped in the knotted net.

A quick, sacred dunk in the Ganges cleanses the grimiest bodies. People wear loose cotton clothes, use no soap and do not scrub dirt from their bodies. The ritual bath purifies even the most recalcitrant sinners. Elbows crunch and poke as men, women and children change out of sopping wet clothes into dry freshly laundered ones.

The *Angrezi* is so absorbed in the panorama of human life and the frenzy of pilgrims standing, dousing and splashing in the river, she doesn't see a monkey jump into the room. Easily he squeezes through the metal bars across one of the open windows. A screech startles her.

"*Chello*! Get Out!" she hisses.

As the monkey turns to leave he picks up the nearest object he can grab, a sandal, then flees. Before the *Angrezi* can hiss again in anger or annoyance, the monkey vanishes like one of the demons who first stole the Pot of Elixir churned from the Ocean of Milk.

She runs to the other window just in time to see the monkey scramble across the courtyard, scale a tree and retreat to an adjacent roof with her sandal in tow.

"My sandal! You wretched thief! My only pair of shoes!"

Human River

The monkey on the neighbor's rooftop bites into the leather sandal then throws the shoe down in disgust. "That bastard! My sandal! My only pair!" The *Angrezi* hobbles to the door.

Before the crowds arrived, to get to the building next door she could exit the building at the street and walk a few paces to the right. In the midst of the *Kumbha Mela* festivities, however, a phenomenal crush of pilgrims fills every inch of space. There is no panic or hysteria. Easily they move together in a singular direction. But the crowd moves in the opposite direction, away from the building where the monkey tossses the sandal.

The crowd is thick. There is no way to reverse directions.

With trepidation the *Angrezi* enters the flow, the tidal wave of people.

Jostle can't describe the claustrophobic press of a religious crowd destined for salvation. The mass overpowers. She can't budge against the immense throng. There is no choice but to blend in, to unite.

A mass of people twenty abreast and a mile long moves like a great centipede with millions of hands and feet. Her body crunches into the pack that flows the wrong way. Trapped in a human river the mass carries her into the swirling chaos.

ROOM WITH A VIEW
OF THE GHATS

The sun sets but the throngs keep swelling. By the time the *Angrezi* comes near the door of the building where the monkey dropped her sandal, she is numbed into disbelief. No sandal, no monkey. Three hours lost in a human river. Three hours that feel like a week.

In utter, exhausted frustration she returns to her perch by the window, relieved to be inside again, yet too stunned to think. The claustrophobic crowds she used to encounter at football stadiums and rock concerts pale next to this congregation. The worshipful crush of pilgrims rub shoulders, shuffle ant-like only inches at a time. Their common goal and unified destination to immerse in the palliative waters of a draining river.

"'Damn that monkey! Why steal a shoe? He can't eat leather!'"

As the midnight hour nears, to be on the safe side, she keeps the remaining sandal near, so she can wield it like a stick and threaten any monkey that might invade the privacy of her room again, the room with a view of the bathing *ghats*.

SACRIFICE

A white-out is an obliteration. In weather it is the state of snow blindness; the chaos of flakes, swirls, and globs of frozen water whipped to a froth. An orgasm is also a white-out, an inundation, an overpowering nullification of externals.

The American's thoughts spin like a vinyl record on the Maharaja's antique hand cranked turntable. Imbibe, inhale, implant, implode, immolate. Buddhist monks in Vietnam set fire to themselves for a cause, to protest oppression or war. Immolation to them is the highest sacrifice because after they sacrifice their body they have nothing left, not even life.

The air in the village thickens. Languid bodies wait for nightfall, for the midnight communal holy convergence.

Even if the American learns the rituals of the country, even if she eats and drinks the food and potions, she is still a foreigner, a *mleccha*, a barbarian. She will never read the secret scriptures stored in the innermost sanctum of the crowded, chaotic sacred temple.

CHARAS WALLAH

The streets of Kathmandu are lined with itinerant street merchants who carry wooden trays supported by leather straps around their necks. They display their wares for all to see: Nepali paper puppets, tie-string cloth purses, popular Ganesh *bidis* hand-rolled in tobacco leaves as well as machine rolled Charminar cigarettes, red and vermillion *tikka* powders and betel nut *pan*. Shoppers crowd the cobblestone alleys too narrow for cars.

There is a sign outside the shop but the *Angrezi* can't read the *devanagari* alphabet. Inside she greets a Nepali man who wears an orange and brown woven *topee* hat, white *kurta* shirt and tightly gathered Nepali *pajamas*—skin tight at the ankle and calf but buoyant and full at the hips and waist.

"*Charas?*" the *Angrezi* asks.

"*Hai.*"

The hashish shop is no hippie head shop. There are no carved wooden or glass pipes, no candies, hash brownies, no potent pot infused sweets or cloyingly scented incense sticks or cones.

The shopkeeper points through a glass counter to the shelf below. Five or six flat bricks of Himalayan hash each a foot long rest side by side. There are no free samples but quality is assured. First class.

The shop keeper points to an indentation in the center of each brick. Every slab is embossed with a stamp of the highest authority: His Majesty, the King of Nepal's royal government seal of approval.

QUANDRY

In the government hash shop as the *Angrezi* stands in front of the glass counter and ponders the government approved grades, she wonders, "First Class or Regular?"

First class, she decides. To herself she mumbles, "What the hell." Then not grinning, not ogling but with a completely straight face bordering on boredom she pretends this is the most common transaction, something like buying a *pow* of *dudh*, a cup of hot boiled milk from a seller's open air cauldron outside on the street.

"*Kitna*? How much?" the merchant asks.

He assembles a handheld set of brass scales. The two dishes on small chains jangle from a handle. He opens a box of tiny brass weights. He sells as little as a *tola* all the way up to a kilo or more.

How much can I carry? the *Angrezi* muses. Enough for a month, a year, for the next ten years? Will I ever find my way back here? Where is here? Where am I? For how long?

Embark, return. Begin, end. Start, finish ...what is the difference? Where is the journey?

SHADY FIGURE

"Half kilo *tik hai*," the *Angrezi* tells the merchant in the *charas* shop.

The *charas wallah* forces the sharp blade of a *gurkha* knife through the inch thick slab of densely packed hash. One half he drops in a brass dish on the scale. Holding the scale aloft he releases brass weights into the other dish. The dish descends lower and lower with each new weight. Both dishes sway, suspended in the air, in balance like breasts in a bra. Using a piece of old newsprint he wraps the block like a fish seller wraps fish at the market, then ties the packet with rough hemp twine.

"A hundred rupees, *memsahib*."

There are no hidden two way mirrors, no telephone taps, no bugs, and no intercepted mail. There is no armed interception, no, "Drop it!!" or "Freeze!!" No frisking, no strip search. No bust, no jail time, no prison sentence or ruined lives.

No shady figure tails her back to her room. Only a stray dog nudges her cloth *jollah* shoulder bag with his nose. The dog fills his nostrils not with the scent of Copenhagen snuff but with the aroma of freshly harvested and dried *charas* that permeates the *Angrezi's* bag like a musky sandalwood perfume.

EARRING

In a pilgrim shelter deep in the Kangra Valley of North India, the *Angrezi* drinks hot, spicy tea she carries in a clay cup from the mountain teashop where every cup takes on the flavor of the wood that boils the brew. Later she bathes in the large hot spring pool at Manikaran, the place where one of the goddess Devi's earrings dropped from the sky after her death.

Her grieving spouse Shiva carried her corpse around for days, too attached to let her go. Loud wails echoed deep into hidden valleys, across seas. Sobs resounded to the bottom of the earth. Too sad to notice, his beloved's body disintegrated, broke into small pieces then fell to the earth beneath him as he wandered blinded by deep sorrow. Where her body parts fell, holy shrines sprang up, worshipped as popular pilgrimage sites. An earring unleashed a gushing hot vapor, steaming bubbles from the earth.

After a hot soak the *Angrezi* climbs down the slippery creek bank. She gingerly balances on mossy stones to reach the icy snowmelt of a stream filled with runoff from the *Gangotri* glacier, a source of the Ganges. Water from the *Dud Kosi*, the River of Milk, bubbles and froths in the shallow creek. To dunk in the cool waters she stretches flat out against the rocks.

The cold assaults her skin with an invigorating tinge.

MARBLE MOUNTAIN

Refreshed after a soak in the hot springs the *Angrezi* hikes back into the Himalayas toward the snow glaciers of Tibet. On a ledge she spreads out a thick woolen blanket and arranges her arms and legs in a yoga posture. Her blanket flaps in the Himalayan winds; hair billows recklessly.

Across the river on the rising slope, pines vigorously shake their limbs one by one, a wild anarchy of arms. Trees animate multi-armed Goddesses whose branches wave with furtive, twisted desire or menace.

The earth radiates in higher altitudes. Clouds roll and tumble in mysterious formations that paint a turquoise sky scented with pine. Giddy with the bliss of altitude, the *Angrezi* stares with amazement at the ground beneath her. She looks closely as if seeing for the first time. Rocks exude the hues and sheen of precious jewels, the beauty of agate veins, quartz and crystal streaks. Rocks sparkle and twinkle like diamonds.

On the walk back she pauses at a vein of black diamonds snaking through a rock face of highly polished marble. She gently strokes the stone like a tame animal. Amazingly the surface vibrates, explodes in a dance of flashing colors.

MULETEER

At the moment the *Angrezi* pauses to admire the jeweled rocks along the mountain trail, a muleteer rounds the bend leading a mule burdened with a top-heavy woven striped bundle tied to his back.

The *Angrezi* watchs them approach. She isn't afraid of the stranger. Rather she recognizes him as a long lost brother, perhaps, or at the very least a fellow traveler on this same mystical mountain path.

She hasn't spoken for days. The few Hindi words she knows are enough to express simple desires or questions in the marketplace. The words that come from her mouth that day surprise her.

"*Bahut acha hai,*" she says in the common Hindi phrase which means simply, "Very, very nice."

The muleteer follows the path of her hand that points at the rock along the path.

Bahut acha hai," she repeats. *Very nice rock. The very best!*

PRETA LOKA

The muleteer who encounters the *Angrezi* stroking the mountain is suspicious. He does not think of her as a sister or a neighbor.

"Why does she stroke the rock?" he wonders. "She says the rock is very nice. What does she mean, very nice? Is she trying to steal my mule? Is she mad? What is so special about the mountain? Rocks are common, nothing special, a convenience only for my mule to piss on. Is she a *Preta* demon from the *Preta Loka?*"

"*Namaste*. Good-day, *memsahib,*" he nods, then as quickly as he can he passes the woman who comes from the other side of the world, two oceans away.

She points again to the rock. "Look at this sparkling, crystal streak. Amazing!"

He nods as if in agreement.

He is lucky, she thinks. What good karma to live in this magical place where rocks explode into colors and cellular specks glisten and pulse.

About twenty-five yards down the trail the muleteer turns around to see if the woman who strokes the stone is real."Is it possible," he wonders, "that somehow I ate a bad mushroom for lunch? Or did I inhale a particularly strong puff of tobacco? Did I imagine the woman? Is the *Angrezi* from the west dressed in a Tibetan *chuba* a figment of my imagination? A crazy high-altitude hallucination? Or is she one of the She-Devils who roam the land masquerading and fooling unsuspecting fools along the trail?

"She is there," he confirms to himself. Then not terribly

curious one way or the other or anticipating arrival rather than departure and the journey in-between, he turns his back to her and continues down the mountain path.

Six
Winners & Losers

FERRET MAN

People call me Ferret Man. I raise ferrets in the yard. They're great hunters and fine pets. My prices are reasonable. My animals well-trained and obedient. Knock at the door some morning and I'll show you my ferrets.

Last summer a housewife came with her milk pail and an empty bowl. She set her bowl down. Poured milk up to the rim.

"Get your ferret," she instructed. "The milk's for him."

"What for?" I asked.

"Just get him. I'll show you."

So I leashed one of my ferrets and brought him to drink. He lapped the milk like it was the finest malt liquor.

"That's it. Enough," the woman said at the halfway mark.

"Let him finish," I said. "No sense wasting milk. No one will drink after a ferret 'cept maybe a cat."

She ignored me and poured the remainder of the milk into a jar and screwed the lid tight.

"It's medicine," she said. "To cure a baby's colic."

Every three weeks she returned. If she wanted to spoil my animal with a bowl of her fresh cow's milk, that was fine with me. I wasn't gonna stop her.

A VERMIN SHOW

In an earlier time before automobiles and sewing machines, the raspy voice of Jack Black plying his wares on the back streets of London rang out in the early mornings: "For Sale! Vermin Bait for Sale! Step Right Here! Two pence to See the Poison Show."

He followed his cry with the echo of a brass bell mounted on his cart: Ding, ding, dinnggg....Clang, dang, donnnggg... "Fast Results! Dozens Killed!"

Some Londoners believed the ubiquitous sewer rats were useful, eating their way through sludge and muck that otherwise festered and oozed in the underground tunnels of the city. Trouble began when the rats left the sewers to wander into homes, taverns, factories, hospitals, and orphanages. Few families and businesses were spared nocturnal visits by voracious rats.

When Jack, a descendant of gypsies, found rat droppings in his favorite suet pudding, he vowed to rid his house of varmints. One homemade vermin pill stopped a huge rat dead in his tracks midway across the kitchen shelf. When a neighbor asked for a sample of his potion Jack's business took off.

On a typical April morning as the fog lifted near the Thames, Jack walked the back streets of London pushing his hand-built cart. Cellar scullery maids and matrons in third story walk-ups, hearing the bell, peered out their doors and windows in time to read "Jack Black Destroyer of Rats" printed on the side of his cart before he wheeled out of view. After walking a few blocks Jack parked the cart and unlocked a small portable stage. To the right of the stage Jack unveiled three cages of rats, a dozen bottles of poisonous pills, and numerous packets of noxious powders.

"These detested vermin—," he began as women, wiping their wet hands on their aprons, came out of their kitchens to watch. "—invade your homes, raid your larders, and breed in your cellars at night."

As he talked he dipped his hand into a cage and pulled out a grungy mud-splattered rat which he set on his sleeve. "They never travel alone. They move in packs and breed like maggots."

Jack's chatter and his rambunctious rats induced other street folks and passersby to stop and look. Men, women and children stared, mouths gaping, as rats, like squirrels in a favorite oak tree, ran up and down Jack's arms. Two rats sat on his shoulders cleaning their faces with their front-paws, poking and sniffing his neck and ears.

One disbeliever whispered to a woman in the crowd, "Bet you those rats are tame. They're no more vicious than ordinary house pets."

While caged the rats led an easy life, free from predators, free from the hustle of sewer life. They enjoyed scampering on cue up the arms and inside the shirt of their master. The highlight of Jack's talk was a performance which started as soon as he drew a crowd of ten.

"Fair ladies and gentlemen...Watch as I place this tiny tablet in the center of the stage."

He pried the cork off of a glass vial filled with round black pills, then scooped out a single pill with his finger and placed it on stage. From the crowd a loud "Ohhh" rang out as Jack plucked a scrawling rat off his sleeve and set him down next to the pill. The rat, unfed for three days and predictably starving, sniffed tentatively, then gobbled down the pill. Jack continued his chatter a few minutes until the audience's attention turned to the rodent which suddenly gagged and twitched as he slipped into the grotesque spasms of an unsightly death.

Cries of "Ahhh..." escaped from the crowd as the doomed rat exhaled his last breath. As Jack flung the carcass toward the street, the crowd hastily cleared a space where it landed with a dull thud.

"A mere two pence buys this poison!" Jack bellowed at the conclusion of each public poisoning. "Lay it about their lairs. Be the killer of vermin. A wise investment today saves money tomorrow. Sell your wares at market price, save it not for rats and mice."

HER MAJESTY'S RAT CATCHER

Jack's mobile Vermin Bait and Rat Show cart brought him plenty of clients, both rich and poor. After he offered a consultation at the royal palace he amended the sign on his cart: "Jack Black, Rat and Mole Destroyer to Her Majesty." He sharpened his attire: black top hat, a top coat with matching black breeches, and a starched white shirt over which he draped a white silk sash embroidered with "Her Majesty's Rat Catcher."

Jack became the most fearless rat handler in all of Britain. He played with his caged rats as if they were blind kittens: he scratched their bellies, rubbed their ears, stroked the fur on their backs, called them names like Poppy, Sachs or Piccadilly.

One customer used a trace of Jack's poison to rid her step-daughter's head of lice. The stepmother—some claimed she had cruel intentions from the beginning—rubbed a small amount crushed into a talc onto the child's scalp. Six days later the poor child died.

"That venomous woman should be tied to a stake," Jack's wife kvetched. "She murdered her own stepdaughter, she did. You be careful with the powders, Jack. Don't inhale them and wash your hands well before supper."

"Don't worry about my safety," he replied. "I never breathe the poison and I don't lick my fingers."

The vermin business was so prosperous Jack retired after five years but before a year passed his body was laid to rest under the ground in a cemetery on the outskirts of the city he helped rid of rodents.

People who valued his services showed little remorse when told of his death. "It takes a rat to catch a rat," one neighbor said. "Rats know the way of rats," another chimed in. Her Majesty's spokesman denied any association with Jack and his rat catching services.

The doctor who examined his body confirmed what Jack's wife suspected all along. Jack's skin absorbed tiny amounts of the poison from the vermin packets he so carefully mixed to sell to street customers. Over time enough poison accumulated in his body to kill him.

RATTING

Like the roar in the coliseum when Romans watched Christians and lions battle, the anxious mayhem of a 19th century Newcastle crowd waiting to witness a ratting match filled the arena and bombarded the ears of the rats waiting to be freed from the confines of overcrowded cages.

In ratting two mismatched contestants, riled and angered by the crowd, flew at each other; they chewed, clawed, bit, ripped flesh and fur. The crowds loved the fast pace: how quickly one beast, the aggressor, the fighter, killed the weaker victim or victims. Blood and guts were an integral part of the game or sport.

To begin a ratting match a boy plunged a hand into the basket cage to catch rats for the pit. A rat may squirm away and elude capture for a match or two but inevitably every rat trapped in the basket ended up in the pit.

A gas lamp suspended over the pit lit the six by six foot arena. As soon as they dropped into the pit, rats raced to the wooden sides. They hated the brightness, the wild noise. A few rats, giddy with the freedom to run after being trapped in the basket, jumped up on their hind legs and tried to climb out of the pit.

Drunken patrons leered at them laughing and cussing. For amusement one lowered his cigar into the pit. When a curious rat sniffed the smoldering tip hoping to find food, he singed his nose.

When too many rats clustered at the corners of the pit, the boy handler forced a blast of air from a huge bellows aimed at the rats.

"Blow them! Blow them!" the audience chanted. Rats hate wind. When wind hit their faces, they reversed directions and fled into the center of the arena which brought lusty cheers from the audience. To a rat a strong facial wind was worse than facing a snarling dog on a killing rampage.

A typical match set a bull terrier against forty rats. When the pit bull attacked, most rats fled to the corners where they pawed over each other on their hind legs trying to climb the walls. A few bold rats met the pit bull head-on. They jumped up into his face, nipped his skin and infuriated him. In the wild, rats sometimes en masse surrounded an enemy like a snake and attacked as a pack. But in the arena the pit bull was too quick for the rats to combat. If a few rats latched onto the dog's snout, he easily shook them off.

Bets were placed on prized champion dogs. One dog thumped a rat in his mouth onto the floor over and over, drumming out a beat.

"He's wasting precious time, he is" one bettor claimed. "Better to keep up the killing. It's the numbers that count the most."

A CHAMPION

In the sport of ratting the dog with the highest body count at the end of a set time—usually eight minutes—won.

A dog's winning strategy consisted of biting a rat and shaking it between his teeth vigorously, then hurling the rat to the floor before scooping up the next rat, and the next, one after the other in rapid succession.

As the dead accumulated, carcasses littered the small pit. After eight minutes a whistle blew, the dog caught and muzzled, the death toll tallied and winning bets paid.

A boy jumped in to sweep aside the dead before the next match began. The remaining rats took a break. Some set about the curious act of preening, or cleaning their faces with their paws as if the business of fighting for their lives had sullied them. A few rats sniffed at the tethered dog to better sense the aggressor, others climbed up the trousers of the boy if he forgot to tie the cuffs to his ankles.

In the annals of ratting the all-time champion was a pit bull named Billy. Some discredited Billy's record—100 rats in eight minutes—but their argument centered on the number of seconds over the eight minutes Billy rampaged. A small quibble his owner said in Billy's defense.

Eventuallly Billy developed a canker in his mouth from a vicious bite. The infection spread until it took over his body. After he died his owner had him stuffed and mounted. For ten years Billy's stuffed display greeted customers at the door of the Seven Bells tavern where Billy's owner was the proprietor.

His demise was a small revenge for the rats, but little compensation for the thousands of rats he massacred to gain his championship title.

The Rat Caterer

Before horse racing and tennis matches, public animal fights, especially bull, bear and dog fights, were popular sporting events that drew large crowds in London. Later the popularity of animal matches declined when the promoters couldn't keep enough of the large animals in stock to satisfy the public's appetite for public fights. Who first introduced the idea of rat fights or ratting made a tidy sum since the sport proved wildly popular in the 1800s. There was no end to the availability of rodents which bred quicker than rabbits.

Everyone from a lowly street urinal sweeper to a high society lady enjoyed the rat pits or rat sports arenas. Hands down people believed rats were the most odious members of the animal kingdom. To see one or a dozen rats viciously and quickly killed had an appeal that the dog or bear matches lacked.

Predictably as the spectator sport of ratting grew in popularity, the demand for live rats increased. And as any market analyst or broker will testify, when and where a demand arose, suppliers soon stepped forward to profit in the trade. Men who had as much cunning and diligence as the original destroyers of rats, turned their attentions to catching, harboring and breeding the rodents. Men like Charlie Brown, a stalwart sort who exhibited the gall and stamina necessary to enter into a verminous trade, enjoyed the rewards of a lucrative livelihood.

Charlie raised both Norwegian rats and black harbor rats in cages behind his house. Within two months after he placed a male and three female rats in a breeding pen, he counted 2,000 rats which ate through, burlap bag and all, a hefty 200 pound sack of barley meal each week. Like any professional breeder, Charlie kept healthy brown and black rats in separate cages.

"Rats of one species do not belong with those of another," he claimed. "If I don't separate them, they'll tear each other to pieces. Barn rats, ship rats or sewer rats never get along."

A few favorite rats lived in fancier cages in his parlor. He invited visitors to tour caged specimens of albino and piebald rats. In one cage a black rat and a white rat, potential parents to a new breed of rats, Charlie hoped, slept at opposite ends.

The caged rats accepted their life of confinement and did not attempt to escape. Parlor rats exhibited no anger. They appeared blind when Charlie pulled them out of their cages but when he finished exhibiting them as soon as the rats neared the cages, they struggled to be set free again—to the freedom they knew—the freedom of confinement.

Every week Charlie delivered a batch of fighting rats to each of eight arenas. Although there were others who supplied fighters for the matches, six months after he started his rat farm Charlie boasted he was the largest rat caterer in the city.

A rat breeder's job was not easy.

"A rat's bite," Charlie said, "was a three cornered one, like a leech's, only deeper and it bled for hours." Dozens of rat bites scarred Charlie's fingers and wrists.

"Charlie, for God's sake!" a friend scolded. "Rub caraway on your fingertips, mate. Or camphor. Don't let them eat you alive."

"Smear dung," his wife suggested. "Rats hate the smell of dung."

"I've rubbed my hands a dozen times," Charlie said, "nothing worked. If a rat wants to bite, he'll bite no matter what balm or repellent I use."

Sometimes one of Charlie's fingers blackened and swelled from a nasty bite. A doctor amputated one finger that turned putrid.

No one said the rat trade was without risk.

Once Charlie attained a modest success in the breeding business, he planned to hire young boys to pull the rats out of the cage for him and drop them into the fighting pit or ring.

Let the boys rub their hands with oils and potions, he mused, maybe the rats won't bite them.

RAT REMEDIES & SUPERSTITIONS

R ATS IN YOUR TREES?
Not all rats live underground. When a tropical South Sea island rat burrows into the sandy dirt, water floods the hole before he can dig a tunnel. Most island rats nest in the waving fronds of coconut trees which provide life's every necessity. Once rats climb the trees, they don't need to come down. When thirsty, they guzzle coconut milk. Sweet coconut meat is their favorite food.

To prevent rats from running up your coconut trees and eating the young coconuts before they have a chance to ripen and drop, fasten a tin funnel-skirt around the swaying tree trunk. A rat's feet will slip on the metal sheet and it will fall back down.

RAT BAIT

In Peking women tell their husbands to place rat poison only in the rat's favorite foods: fried cakes and desserts, fruits and radishes. If they put the poison in cold noodles, rice or leftover wontons they'll risk wasting both the leftover food and the poison.

DOMESTIC DISPUTE

A mother rat fiercely protects her young, blinded, hairless rat babies after birth. Not even the father rat is allowed near the babies. The mother doesn't trust a male's voracious appetite. Some rat fathers are rumored to have eaten their offspring. If a father rat insists on seeing his rat children, an argument with the mother rat may ensue. Arguments lead to fights.

If the mother rat kills the father rat, her act is considered self-defense. She may drink from his blood once his body is inert before her, but her primary actions are driven by a maternal rather than a cannibalistic instinct.

CARNIVORES

In the underground world of rats, if a rat gets caught in a trap or dies, other rats think nothing of devouring the victim: warm blood and brains are especially prized morsels.

Be careful then when digging up a rat's nest. Rats not only bite, they relish flesh and blood of all types.

RAT PREDATORS

To eliminate rats at home, natural rat predators make excellent pets. Set a pet cobra loose in the garden and a python in the basement. Snakes will feed on any rats that approach from the outside or tunnel through to the basement. Ferrets or weasels work well as house pets and can patrol inside the house.

CARGO RATS

A sea captain once lowered an alligator into his ship's hold. Thinking the alligator would quickly feed on the multitude of rats hiding in the bowels of the ship, he confidently set sail with a full cargo. His plan worked for two weeks but then the alligator died of dehydration. The rats feasted on the corpse. With the abundant food source provided by the alligator, compliments of the captain, the rats soon exceeded their original numbers.

Look Before You Sit

When the sludge and muck levels run low in the underground sewers, rats searching for new sources of food, start swimming through sewer pipes.

Most household drain pipes have traps too small for a rat to swim through.

Occasionally a rat pawing through a cess pool or treading through sewage water finds a drain opening large enough to squeeze through. Taking a deep breath, a rat, which can hold its breath for three full minutes, heads for the brightest source of light—the light from the large opening of a common toilet bowl.

To prevent surprise rat bites especially in the tenderest of areas, "Keep the toilet seat down until needed," a plumber recommends. "And look before you sit."

Poison

The best time to kill moles and water rats, according to one English gardener, is in March and September when they breed. His recipe to get rid of rats: mix green powdered glass and sweetened desiccated coconut into a paste. Set out small half inch balls of the concoction as bait near a rat colony. The rats love coconut and will greedily gobble any left out. Their stomachs, however, can't digest glass. Glass settles into their bowels and intestines. Every move a rat makes after swallowing glass perforates the guts. Within a week the rat bleeds to death from internal wounds.

Rat Packs

Never fight a rat pack alone. The behavior of marauding rats is unpredictable. A quick, brave—or desperate—snake that blindly pokes a head into a rat burrow may be in for a big suprise. Single rats, if confronted by a large predator, flee. But en mass rats can attack people and large animals, including their own predators without the slightest hesitancy.

TOOTHACHE

To cure a child's toothache, throw an extracted baby tooth onto a thatched roof where rats nest. They'll find the tooth and gnaw on it. Rats have teeth so hard they can chew through metal. When rats gnaw on the discarded child's tooth all pains and aches will disappear.

WHISKERS

To grow a full beard with long hair as strong as rat whiskers, prick the chin all over with a sharpened rat bone. Then rub the tiny sores with a stone taken from a rat's den and imbued with the power of a rat soul.

RAT NEEDLES

Use the sharpened bone of a rat as a tattoo needle. Tattoo colors will seep deep under a skin that is punctured by a rat needle. Just as a rat penetrates the dark interior of the earth—rat colors—green, brown, blue and violet, penetrate the skin. If a tattoo artist uses rat bone needles the color will never fade or wash out.

RAT EVOLUTION

One scientist's theory of evolution blamed rats for the end of the dinosaur era. Eons ago, the theory goes, the rat population exploded out of control. Rats multiplied and ate all the vegetation in the forests, fields and swamps. Rats ate fish, birds and snakes; they ate wood, fruits and bugs. Since every edible leaf, root and branch soon disappeared, there was not enough food left for the vegetable-loving dinosaurs to eat to fill their immense stomachs so they died out.

RAT SCIENCE

A scientist analyzed glossy black clumps of rat piss and dung dug up from an ancient underground rat nest. She presented field data that detected the effect of cosmic rays hitting the earth, traced the magnetic fields and charted erratic weather patterns in ancient times.

"Rat piss can predict the weather," she concluded, "if it crystallizes and ages for 40,000 years."

OTHER VERMIN
REMEDIES & SUPERSTITIONS

**

To reduce the number of lice in the hair, an old herbal suggests this cure: gather fresh parsley from the garden in the fall after the plant has gone to seed. Pound the parsley seed into a fine powder and rub it into the roots of the hair. If the lice do not disappear after the first application; repeat as often as necessary.

**

Women in medieval France dangled flea traps from the enormous wire hoops they wore under their long skirts. The traps were dainty little ceramic sachet pots with tiny holes in the top. The fleas, attracted to the scent of honey inside the pot, crawled in through the holes. Once inside the fleas' feet stuck in the honey and they couldn't jump back out again. Fleas suffocated and drowned a sticky honey death.

**

After there is a surprise snowfall in May, if an Ozark housewife melts some of the snow in the fireplace, fleas and bedbugs will leave her home. Or she can bring a sheep into the house for a few days: make the animal a comfy bed by the fireplace. Give the fleas a day or two to find the sheep.

Fleas love lamb's wool. When she leads the sheep back outside all the fleas will be hiding in the wool.

**

Children will not be troubled with worms if they chew the turpentine-like resin from pine wood. A good time to catch the resin is when the wood is set near the heat of a fire.

**

To rid a cabin of fleas and bedbugs sprinkle splinters from a tree struck by lightning. After sniffing the wood, a flea sensing the tree's violent fiery lightning death will quickly flee the cabin.

**

Ladies, do not let your hairdresser coif your hair in a beehive bun. Black widow spiders love to nest in the hollow caverns of teased and ratted hair. If a spider picks your head to build a nest in, you can die from the poisonous sting of a black widow's bite.

**

In the woods if a leech bites, yank it off the skin immediately. If the leech is firmly attached sprinkle a little salt on the slimy surface and wait. The salt stings so bad, a leech, like a banana slug, turns inside out trying to find relief.

**

In the old days people kept pet leeches for medicinal purposes, especially to use for blood-letting and to suck out the poison from insect or snake bites.

To keep leeches: store them in a glass jar with an air hole in the lid and a small piece of moss at the bottom. Cover with a piece of damp muslin. Keep in a darkened cupboard. After a leech is allowed to feed and falls off the patient chock full of blood, take it by the tail. Slowly draw the leech through the thumb and finger to thoroughly press out all the blood from a leech's stomach. Then he'll be ready for the next job.

**

To subdue ants infiltrating a kitchen, one Cockney man sets out a basin of syrup made from beer and sugar. He places little wooden planks to help the ants get up the sides of the basin. Once they fall into the syrup, they can't get back out again.

**

A Zen Buddhist leaves a bowl of sugar outside his kitchen.

"Ants love sugar," he explains. "If they satisfy their craving outside first, they don't need to come inside the kitchen."

**

One way to slow down infestations of vermin is to capture their eggs and larva before they hatch into countless little vermin. It's easier to do away with batches of mosquito larvae, for instance, than to single out and kill the grown mosquitoes, one by one.

Mosquitoes breed in standing water. During the rainy season mosquitoes lay their larvae in lakes and ponds. The more water that remains standing above ground, the greater the chances it will soon swarm with larvae. Few mosquitoes survive during drought years.

**

Mosquito caviar was an ancient, pre-Hispanic delicacy. In the cool of a dawn morning carefully gather the larvae soon after a mother mosquito deposits it.

To prepare the thousand year old Mayan dish called *ahuautle*: Use a giant strainer to strain excess water out of the waterborne larvae. Refrigerate until ready to serve. To cook stir two egg yolks into the dusty mosquito caviar to form a creamy paste. Pour the batter into a frying pan and cook like pancakes.

**

If you ask a spouse or friend to pluck the lice out of your hair, do not let them kill the vermin. Kill your own lice. The same holds true for fleas, bedbugs, ticks and mosquitoes. If someone else kills the vermin their fingers will be soiled with your blood which could be used in witchcraft ceremonies without your knowledge.

**

The *sadhus* of India rub ash from cremation pyres onto their skin as an act of worship. A beneficial side effect, *sadhus* claim, is ash rubbed into the scalp repels and suffocates lice. This is lucky since lice love *sadhus'* long, matted dreads. If a *sadhu* tries to use a small fine-toothed lice comb to pick the nits from his hair, he will never comb through the yard long dreadlocks. Tantric *sadhus* prefer human ash but any ash will work.

**

A gardener at Says-Court England suggests gardeners pour the finest bottled English ale into wide-mouthed glasses and "sweeten with a little honey or sugar" to keep flies, wasps, and ants out of the garden."This works for snails and slugs, too," he says. The pests greedily guzzle the fermented beer. But when they bend over the rim of a wide-mouthed glass, they fall into the beer and can't hop or crawl out again. When they try, their feet slip on the glass rim. They drowned drinking themselves into oblivion with the sweetened alcohol.

**

One Manhattan couple keep a live iguana in their apartment. They do not feed the pet but turn him loose at night to stalk and prey on unsuspecting cockroaches in their kitchen.

**

Avoid bedbugs by not sleeping in cheap rundown hotels. Also do not sleep in pilgrim sheds, caravansaries, or wayside hostels where scruffy travelers frequent. "Don't walk barefoot in strange motels," a father warns his son. "Sleep in your socks, too. Scabies, athlete's foot and mange— sneaky vermin you can't even see, are just waiting for a chance to land on some nice young man's foot."

**

To deter cockroaches: sprinkle a small ring of baking soda around every water faucet and the toilet, too. On the way to getting a drink, the cockroach encounters the ring of soda and eats some. Then when the roach takes a drink, the water interacts with the soda and causes the roach's stomach to explode.

**

Chiggers native to the West Indies like to burrow beneath a man's skin. A favorite nesting place is under a toe nail where a single chigger can grow unnoticed to the size of a pea. If a chigger digs into your toe, act quickly to root out the vermin before thousands of eggs or nits hatch. Hold a match close to the skin to sweat the chigger out.

One soldier waited too long after a chigger burrowed in. The only remedy the doctor had was to amputate the sole of the soldier's foot before the infestation spread to his ankle and calf.

**

Some weavers specialize in spinning and weaving dog and cat hair. Their customers are pet owners who want mementos of their pets. To gather enough hair for the weaver to make a small sweater or scarf, the owner collects fur balls and loose hair plucked from the teeth of a pet brush or comb. It takes months and even a year to gather enough hair and fur. When the owner brings the odd fur balls and loose hair en masse to the weaver, before carding and spinning it into dog or cat hair yarn, the smart weaver puts the hair in the freezer for two weeks. The subzero temperature kills any flea larvae.

**

Natural roach repellents: sliced cucumbers placed in a cupboard repels cockroaches. Be careful to replace after two days or you will attract fruit flies. Also small packets of crushed dried leaves from the bay tree will discourage roaches from entering a drawer or cupboard.

**

A mother told her daughter: "When I was a girl we lived in the country. The dogs brought home lots of fleas. Many fleas found their way into my bed. Oh, I hated that itching and scratching. I could hardly sleep at nights my skin burned so.

To get rid of those bastards, I slipped out of bed late at night, quickly in the dark. Carefully I bunched the sheets up with the fleas inside. I filled the bathtub full of water and shook out the sheets over the water. The fleas, every last one of them, fell into the water and drowned."

**

Hungarian shepherds rub hog fat into their clothes to keep the fleas away. The English throw fistfuls of wormwood around their bed chambers before going to sleep.

**

Queen Christina of Sweden once took quick aim at the fleas in her royal bed and fired two rounds with a piece of artillery. The weaponry she used is displayed in Stockholm's Royal Arsenal.

ITCHY SCALP

A washerman named Dhobi, who lived near the Ganges in Varanasi, tried every medication sold in the local dispensary to get rid of itchy scalp: Ayurvedic preparations, homeopathic concoctions, castor oil, linseed oil, mustard powder. He even tried yogic exercises such as standing on his head for ten minutes three times a day. When his hair started to fall out he had a good excuse to visit the local herb doctor. But even the doctor couldn't stop that exasperating itch.

"Dandruff! It must be dandruff! the doctor concluded, handing Dhobi yet another gooey cream rinse.

Dhobi dutifully took the bottle down to the river and bathed in the usual way, following up with applying the rinse to his hair. It was so slimy, however, he had trouble rinsing the lotion out of his hair. River silt clung to the strands. He had to buy a small-toothed comb to ply his way through the mess.

It was then that Dhobi made a startling discovery. Ambling down between the teeth of the comb was a large chunk of dandruff. Dhobi looked closer.

"Ah-ha!" he exclaimed. "Head lice! I should have known."

A special lice treatment was available in the bazaar. For twenty-five paisa Dhobi could rent a monkey on a leash. The monkey meticulously picked through his scalp singling out the vermin and expertly popped them into his mouth. With smacking lips, the monkey scrunched the lice between his teeth like pomegranate seeds, juice squirting all over.

Acknowledgements

For Donald Barthelme (1931-1989) or Uncle Don, as he asked students to call him, who was a mentor at the University of Houston. His exemplary work, perspicacious wit, wisdom and encouragement are a continual source of inspiration.

Grateful acknowledgment is made to the editors and publishers of the following magazines and journals where stories, some in earlier versions, were first published:

"Street Show" in ZYZZYVA

"The Rat Caterer," "Rat Currency" and "Rat Tavern" in *Gargoyle Magazine*

"House of Glass" in *Kes5tra*

"The House of Fleas" in *Exquisite Corpse*

"The Rat Queen," "The Rat Tax," and "A Rat Scam" in *North American Review*

"Rat Fishing in Ohio" in *The Woodstock Journal*

"Remedies & Superstitions" in *Raven Chronicles*

Six excerpts from "The Rat Chronicles" in Nico Morrison's "The Art of Writing" blog.

Earlier versions of a few of the stories appeared in two privately printed chapbooks: *Vermin: A Bestiary* (Reservoir Press, NY) and *The Monkey Thief* (Shivastan Publishers, Kathmandu, Nepal.) Versions of a few tales previously appeared in *The Census Taker: Tales of a Traveler in India and Nepal; Travelers' Tales Nepal: True Stories of Life on the Road;* and *Sleeping in Caves: A Sixties Himalayan Memoir.*

Many thanks to Anne Depue for encouragement, insightful readings, editorial suggestions and author representation and to Mary Bisbee-Beek for inspiration, editorial support, publisher expertise and publicity savvy. A few tales were inspired by the writings and observations of J. Henri Fabre, Francis Burkland and Henry Mayhew.

MARILYN STABLEIN is an award-winning poet, essayist, fiction writer and mixed media artist whose sculptural artist's books, altered books and performance art concern visual narrative, travelog and memoir.

Her books include *Houseboat on the Ganges & A Room in Kathmandu*; *Night Travels to Tibet*; *Sleeping in Caves: A Sixties Himalayan Memoir*; a collection of eco-essays set in the Northwest, *Climate of Extremes: Landscape and Imagination*; *Splitting Hard Ground: Poems* (New Mexico Book Award) and *Bind, Alter Fold*, a monograph of her artist books.

Her collages, assemblages and artist books are exhibited internationally and are in private and public collections including: SUNY Buffalo, Yale University Beinecke Library, Brown University Library, The British Library and University of Washington, Suzallo and Allen Libraries Special Collections.

She lives and teaches in Portland, Oregon.

Visit: marilynstablein.com